# reinvent

*start fresh and love life!*

**beth jones**

New York  Nashville

FaithWords
Hachette Book Group
1290 Avenue of the Americas, New York, NY 10104
faithwords.com
twitter.com/faithwords

First edition: May 2020

FaithWords is a division of Hachette Book Group, Inc. The FaithWords name and logo are trademarks of Hachette Book Group, Inc.



LCCN: 2019956960

ISBNs: 978-1-5460-1725-7 (hardcover), 978-1-5460-1727-1 (ebook)

Printed in the United States of America

LSC-C

10 9 8 7 6 5 4 3 2 1

# contents

## PART 2: LOVE LIFE!
## 4 QUESTIONS TO REINVENT YOUR LIFE

*To my single mother, Carol Barker—now enjoying heaven!*
*You blazed an amazing reinvention trail*
*and showed us four girls how to start fresh and love life!*
*You've always been my hero and I can't wait to see you again!*
*Love you, Mom!*

*To all you single moms—*
*who work tirelessly to give your kids the best life has to offer;*
*who pray diligently and make sacrifices every day;*
*who burn the candle at both ends and stretch every penny out of every dollar;*
*who work miracles with a can of tuna and a box of mac and cheese;*
*and who have hearts as big as the world—*
*your love, strength, and faith are making a difference for your kids!*
*May you be blessed as you reinvent: Start fresh and love life!*
*You have my love and highest admiration!*

# introduction

> ***Reinvent:*** *(verb)*
> *Change (something) so much that it appears to be entirely new.*
>
> Lexico

Why a book on reinventing yourself, starting fresh, and loving life? As a pastor and mentor, I've ministered to thousands of people over the past thirty years, and I've noticed something. Many people feel stuck or wonder why they aren't further along at this point in their lives. Others are taking stock of their lives and trying to figure out what they want to be "when they grow up" or how to make more of a difference.

It seems like everyone would like to reinvent, redo, or reset some area of their lives. And here's the thing—those who believe they can reinvent their lives, do.

But what do these people have that you don't? Are they more spiritual, talented, connected, or gifted? Absolutely not! Maybe they've just been empowered with the right tools, they believed they could, and they decided to go for it?

## INTRODUCTION

### god is for you!

With God on your side, you can reinvent—no matter what season you're in or what challenge you're facing. It's time to obliterate the gap between where you are now and where you want to be. That's why this book is loaded, not with the greatest sounding theories, but with proven strategies and dozens of "ah-ha" moments that will reignite your passion for life, empower you to realize your full potential, and equip you to start living in your God-given purpose! Whether the canvas of your life is spotless or splattered with paint of every color, you really can *Reinvent: start fresh and love life!*

How do I know?

Not only have I witnessed firsthand in others what God can do, but also He has been reinventing my life for the past forty years. (He's had a lot to work with!) From my first experiences with a bully in kindergarten to my parents' split when I was eight and then being raised by a single mom; to walking two miles to church in search of God; to years of feeling rejected and unwanted as a teenager and young adult; to a bit of persecution as the first believer in my family; to criticism as a woman in church leadership; to the craziness of raising four kids and the pressures of pioneering a church; to thyroid cancer and the health challenges that came from a whacked-out parathyroid; to the heartbreak of betrayals when I least expected it; to feeling overlooked and hidden while my dreams were deferred yet again; and to the normal challenges of life, marriage, family, finances, and ministry—I can tell you now, the Lord has done more than I could have thought of or asked for in every area of my life. I am living proof—as are many others—that God is still in the reinventing business!

I know the Lord wants the same for you!

That's my goal—and the reason—for this book!

I've been praying for you, and I want to empower you with practical solutions, positive inspiration, and the biblical wisdom you need to reinvent your life! Every time I sat down to write, with my tall Americano (coffee drink, not my six-foot-six husband) and laptop, I asked the Lord for the right words, for the right stories, and for all the dots to connect to help you *reinvent*!

## reinventing yourself is fun!

I first taught these principles twenty years ago to a group of 500 Christian entrepreneurs, inventors, and creators, as one of the speakers at a leadership conference. I have since taught them many times to college students, conference attendees, on television, and to the church family that my husband and I pastor. I love to watch what God does as people get ahold of these principles.

I don't want to sugarcoat it: Reinventing yourself is fun, and it works—but it won't just happen by hoping for it or looking for good vibes. There's no Tinker Bell dust to "throw around like confetti" for instant results. (But you already know that—that's why you have this book in your hands.) Reinvention is a strategic, intentional faith adventure, and by following the step-by-step plan God has revealed in His Word and throughout this book, you will be able to create your own customized reinvention roadmap to experience it!

You can reinvent your happiness. Your family. Your friendships. Your success. Your income. Your impact. Your health. Your relationship with the Lord. Your satisfaction. And so much more…

## what will this book do for you?

At the heart of this book is the unwavering belief that you can reinvent any area of your life. In every chapter, you will find the ingredients you need to make your own reinvention secret sauce, as well as markers for plotting out your own game plan.

You'll receive fresh revelation, practical how-tos, and dozens of innovative ideas for transforming your life in a holistic way—spirit, soul, and body.

You'll receive wisdom from God's Word as well as the real-life stories of those who have put these principles to work in both sacred and secular arenas. I'll also reveal the personal, awkward, and embarrassing reinvention lessons I've learned along the way—proven, time-tested principles that I am happy to share with you!

Let me give you a sneak peek into where we're going...

In Part 1 of the book, I will introduce you to the 4 Reasons to Reinvent Your Life. As we take our time to unpack each reason, you will receive loads of revelation and motivation to help you reinvent your life in a systematic, God-touched way. We'll cover these four reasons:

*Reinvent Reason #1: The Gaps*
*Reinvent Reason #2: The Crossroads*
*Reinvent Reason #3: The Future*
*Reinvent Reason #4: The Love*

Each reason we discuss will answer nagging questions you may have about the current state of your life, and they will empower and bolster your internal resolve to reinvent. By taking our time to carefully examine the reasons to reinvent, you will have a better understanding of your starting point,

and this will be an important key to your reinvention. Not only that, but also by giving your attention to each one of these reasons to reinvent, you will strengthen your foundation for a reinvention that will last.

In Part 2 of the book, we will get very practical as I help you answer the 4 Questions to Reinvent Your Life. These questions are found embedded in the Bible, within the story of a remarkable, widowed, single mom of two boys (whom we will affectionately call the Maven). She experienced a phenomenal God-touched reinvention by answering these four questions and so will you.

*Reinvent Question #1: What do you want?*
*Reinvent Question #2: What do you have?*
*Reinvent Question #3: What will you do?*
*Reinvent Question #4: Why will you do it?*

Consider this book your personal handbook, cookbook, and field guide. I believe the Lord will speak to your heart with His wisdom and witty ideas as you read each chapter.

### for those new to me, here's a quick introduction

I'm a gal from Kalamazoo! (It's true, and also—for those over fifty—a hat tip to the Glenn Miller song!) I've been a follower of Jesus for the past forty years (Best. Reinvention. Ever.) and I'm passionate about helping people know Him. I've been married to my husband, Jeff, for over thirty years, and we have four adult kids, all of whom are married to amazing people we affectionately call our "in-loves." The grandbaby season has just begun, and at the moment we have two sweet grandbabies.

For the past thirty years, in addition to raising our four kids, I have served in ministry working alongside Jeff. It's been a wild ride and a faith adventure, often with only one nostril above water, but by God's grace, we pioneered and pastor Valley Family Church—a megachurch in a small community with some of the most amazing people in all of Southwest Michigan. Along the way, I've written twenty books to help people "get a grip" on the Bible basics, and these days, we air *The Basics With Beth* TV program around the world on traditional and smart TV platforms.

## i'll be over here cheering you on . . .

While we may never actually meet in person, through the miracle of the written page and the prayers that have gone with this book I'll be like the wild mom in the bleachers hollering, "You can do this! You've got it! C'mon, keep going! I'm so proud of you!" (And, when you're tempted to give up, I'll be here to give you the "No more whining, Cupcake! Don't quit now!" pep talk.) *#highfivesallaround*

You are filled with incredible God-given potential, and with God on your side, your reinvention is possible! Whether you want to revive dormant dreams or aim for new aspirations, or whether you're facing an old or an unexpected challenge, dealing with change, or just need an upgrade in life, you can tap into God's power to make things entirely new. You can reinvent. You can start fresh. You can love life!

Let's pray, so you can get started!

*Father, I pray for every person reading this book. I ask You to help them to reinvent their lives—empower them to start fresh and love life, according to Your will. I pray You give them the wisdom*

*and revelation they need to reach their greatest God-given potential. And... I ask You to pour out a fresh anointing of joy upon them in the process! May eternal fruit be the result of our time together in these pages. In Jesus's mighty name, amen!*

God has heard our prayer! Here we go...

part 1: start fresh!

# 4 reasons to reinvent your life

section 1

# reinvent reason #1: *the gaps*

## chapter 1

# the gap is real

> *You can't go back and change the beginning, but you can start where you are and change the ending.*
>
> C. S. Lewis

I was pregnant with our fourth child. The water in the tiny rented cottage we called home smelled like sulfur (i.e., rotten eggs) and was loaded with so much iron it had the hair of our three ultra-blond-headed kids (and their toenails) turning orange. We were planting a church, raising toddlers, living on Barely-Get-Along Street, and living in an extremely difficult season of reinvention. I blamed my husband for our predicament—after all, it had to be someone's fault. (Smile.)

My husband slept in the "attic-like" loft, and the kids were in a makeshift closet-turned-bedroom. I had the one microscopic bedroom all to myself because I was pregnant and hormonal and huge—and we weren't in a "let's spoon" season.

Meanwhile, we were pioneering our beloved Valley Family Church and had put all of the money we had from our savings and retirement (it wasn't much) into planting the church. The church launched, but she didn't explode with growth

overnight—no, she was on the "turtle plan" and grew ever so slowly.

The gap was real! Meaning, there was a huge gap between the *ideal* life we envisioned and the *real* life we were living.

In our *ideal* life, we were a happy couple, apparently having good sex and popping out a baby every two years! We envisioned our idyllic life—a loving family living in a four-bedroom house on a lake and driving around town in our customized conversion van while belting out *VeggieTales* praise songs with the kids. We loved pastoring a healthy church in Kalamazoo and wouldn't you know...just like the apostle Paul in Antioch, "the whole city came to hear the Word"—because, geez, we weren't building a monument. This was a movement!

In our *ideal* world, all of this was happening.

Plus, we lived a balanced life and Jesus was glorified, on earth as it is in heaven. Yes, amen!

In our *real* life, Jeff and I were in separate rooms and our kids had orange stinkin' toenails! We didn't have two nickels to rub together. Our Suzuki Sidekick didn't have enough seat belts for our entire family and our rented home (what we affectionately called the sulfur pit) was disgusting. Our first church leadership team might have been part of a witness protection program (sorta ~~kidding~~).

We hadn't slept through the night for God knows how long and we were mainlining coffee. We weren't praying for Jesus to be glorified; we were praying for Jesus to come get us!

When "Thou shalt deliver my soul from hell" (Psalm 16:10) was our go-to comfort verse, we knew we had troubles in River City!

Yep, there was a gap!

It was a rough time, and it was going to take years of God's reinventing work to give us the wisdom, maturity, and *sleep* we

needed to experience the good fruit we knew He wanted to grow in and through our lives.

There. Do you feel better? I hope so.

I know we all have our stories. And it's our stories—and the gaps—that remind us of our need to reinvent. Why reinvent? Because the gap is real!

## the gap

There is a gap in our lives when our *ideal* self and our *real* self seem to be miles apart. The gap can exist in any area of our lives where we're dissatisfied or feel we're missing the mark. The gap is the difference between what we envisioned our life would look like by now and what it actually looks like.

the gap

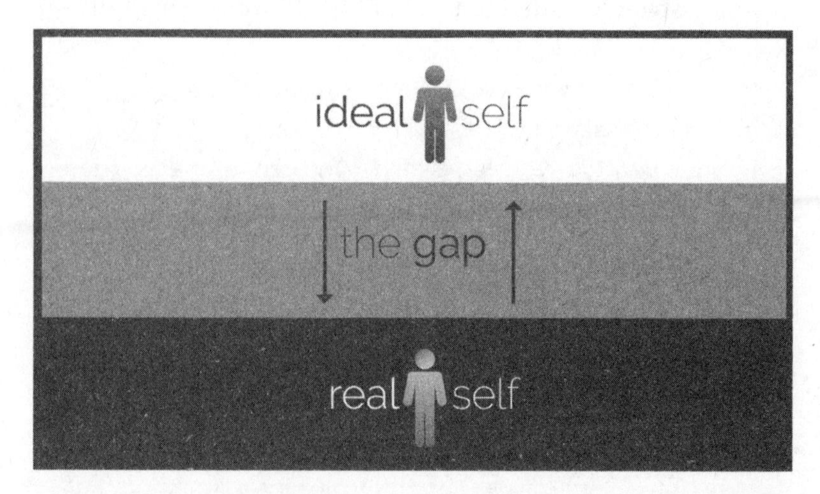


In other words, have you ever thought, *By this time in my life, I expected to be here or there*... or *By now I thought I would have*

*accomplished this or done that*...? The distance between your *ideal* self (who you thought you would be) and your *real* self (who you actually are) is the gap.

The good news is that with God's help we can reinvent our lives and close the gap. We're going to spend a few chapters talking about the gap and identifying where it shows up in our lives.

Being honest about our gaps is a critical first step in the reinvention process.

## hope deferred

The gap is when your hopes are deferred again and yet again. The gap between your *ideal* life and your *real* life can be very disheartening. The writer of Proverbs captured this perfectly:

> **Hope deferred** makes the heart sick,
> **but a dream fulfilled** is a tree of life. (Proverbs 13:12 NLT)

*Hope deferred* is when your hopes, dreams, desires, goals, and vision seem to take forever!

In your *ideal* life you hope for it, you see it, and you've believed, prayed, fasted, confessed, pedaled, worked, served, and faithfully done all you know to do—for three years or maybe three decades—to see it realized.

Yet, in your *real* life, you're dismayed, disappointed, and heartsick, because these things have not yet materialized. When you're still waiting for your time, your mate, your baby, your open door, your opportunity, your success, your miracle, or your big break, it's easy to slip into self-pity, depression, anger, despair, and jealousy—especially as you watch everyone else soar to the heavens with their dreams.

And if you're honest, you're just a little perturbed with God and everybody else.

A *dream fulfilled* is when at last your goal is reached! Your vision has come to pass. God has opened doors. Your time has come. Business is booming. Your mate has arrived. The baby is on the way. Divine connections are happening. You've got favor. You are at the right place at the right time. This is a tree of life and the fruit—spirit, soul, and body—is delicious!

The gap between *hope deferred* and a *dream fulfilled* is a big deal. Whether it's in every area of your life or in the one area most important to you, when fruit is hard to come by, the delay can be crushing.

If you are in this "hope deferred" season and feeling fruitless, it's easy to become very discouraged and tempted to quit everything! But don't...the Lord wants to encourage you!

This reminds me of Jesus's Parable of the Fruitless Tree.

> He also spoke this parable:
>
> A certain man had a fig tree planted in his vineyard, and he came seeking fruit on it and found none.
>
> Then he said to the keeper of his vineyard, "Look, for three years I have come seeking fruit on this fig tree and find none. Cut it down; why does it use up the ground?"
>
> But he answered and said to him, "Sir, let it alone this year also, until I dig around it and fertilize it. And if it bears fruit, well. But if not, after that you can cut it down." (Luke 13:6–9)

While the Parable of the Fruitless Tree may have prophetic inferences, it definitely has practical implications and serves as a great metaphor for us.

Let's replay the story.

Jesus said the vineyard owner (God, the Father) came seeking fruit on his fig tree and found none! The Lord wants His trees (you and me) to be fruitful. This tree had all the potential in the world to produce fruit and yet, year after year, it did not.

Finally, after three years of fruitlessness, the vineyard owner said, "Cut it down!"

That's when the gardener (Jesus) piped up, "Wait! Let's give it one more year! Let me *reinvent* it by digging around the roots and fertilizing it—and if it doesn't produce fruit, then you can cut it down."

Jesus didn't give up on the tree. He wanted it to produce fruit and He was convinced a lot could happen in one year. That's encouraging for us!

Do you feel like the fruitless tree? Whether in your spiritual life and sense of destiny, your physical health, your business and financial welfare, or in your relationships? If you see a gap between the fruit of the *ideal* life you envisioned and the fruit in the *real* life you're living, Jesus wants to help you dig around the roots and fertilize to produce more fruit! (*#reinvent!*)

## be fruitful

Let's talk about fruit. Fruit is an interesting thing. Think about it. The first words God ever spoke to mankind way back in Genesis were "Be fruitful and multiply."

Of all the words God could have chosen, of all the phrases He could have spoken, why this phrase? He could have said, "Welcome to earth!" Or, "Hey, humans, I love you." Or, "Be nice."

Instead, His command to "be fruitful and multiply" reminds us of the God-given drive for fruit, increase, reproduction, growth, and impact that He put on the inside of every person!

He has created us to produce fruit—whether in producing more children, growing more crops, building a business, or multiplying our influence. We have a God-given desire to "be fruitful and multiply."

And, not just a little bit—God put big dreams within us!

That's why we dislike not being fruitful. That's why fruitlessness is a big deal.

The desire for temporal fruit, success, and influence compels us—but there is an eternal desire within us, too. We don't just want to make a dent in the universe; we want to produce fruit that will put a dent in eternity.

God wants that for us, too! He wants our lives to be fruitful—He wants us to enjoy fruit in this life and produce fruit that will last for eternity.

When there is a gap in the fruitfulness of our lives, we are not satisfied. So, what kind of fruit is the Lord interested in? Thankfully, He defined it for us.

First, there's the fruit of the Spirit: "But the Holy Spirit produces this kind of fruit in our lives: **love, joy, peace, patience, kindness, goodness, faithfulness, gentleness, and self-control.** There is no law against these things!" (Galatians 5:22–23 NLT). As God reinvents our lives, we should see an increasing harvest of the fruit of the Spirit.

Second, there's the fruit of eternal influence. Jesus said, "You didn't choose me, but I've chosen and commissioned you to **go into the world to bear fruit.** And your fruit will last, because whatever you ask of my Father, for my sake, he will give it to you!" (John 15:16 TPT). Nothing is more fulfilling than reinventing our lives to close the gap and produce this kind of lasting fruit.

However, fruitfulness is not always an easy process.

Friends of ours who own a large commercial greenhouse

business described it this way. In the perfect climate of the greenhouse where they can control the temperature, water, light, and nutrients, plants flourish! (If only life were that way.) In the greenhouse, they can plant, plan, and prepare for growth and fruitfulness, but they cannot force the process.

Well, sort of...

Our friends told us they *could* "force grow" a tomato plant with fertilizer—but, in doing so, it would never produce fruit! The plant would grow quickly and shoot straight up. It would look like a tomato plant and smell like a tomato plant, but it would *never* produce one tomato—the very purpose for which is was created! (That's a big gap!)

They explained it this way—when the plant is forced to grow too fast, the short little roots do not have time to develop, and as a result the plant appears to be mature but is unable to produce fruit.

Thankfully, the Lord won't "force grow" us to close the gaps in our life. (Ever noticed? God is not in a hurry.) He won't speed things up to our detriment and fruitlessness! The Lord won't cut corners for quick gains—He wants to produce real fruit in our lives. (We'll talk more about that in the next chapter.)

Why reinvent? Because we all have gaps between our *ideal* life and our *real* life. Because our hopes have been deferred for some time and we're ready to taste the tree of life. Because we want to see more fruit in our lives. Yep, there's one simple reason to reinvent: *The gap is real!*

## reinvention review

1. How does the idea that *the gap is real* impact your desire to reinvent your life?
2. How would you describe the gap between your *real* life and *ideal* life at this time?
3. In what ways do you feel your hopes have been deferred and/or how do you relate to the Parable of the Fruitless Tree?

# chapter 2

# the fruit is sparse

> *Let's face it. It's taken years for you to learn to be the person you are, so you're not going to change overnight. But the good news is that you can unlearn those aspects that you want to change and chart a new path in life. And it's never too late to start, whether you're twenty, forty, sixty, or eighty!*
>
> Kevin Leman

I did a very nonofficial survey on my Instastory and asked, "If you were able to get a life 'do-over,' what would you most want to 'do over' or change?"

The honest answers I received were interesting and heartfelt.

- *I would be myself sooner. When you're young it's difficult to be happy with who you are because you are trying to fit in or not draw attention to yourself.* —Age 26
- *I wouldn't be as introverted and always quiet. I end up losing friends.* —Age 17
- *Take more risks big and small.* —Age 32
- *I would have let my kids eat peanut butter and jelly for breakfast,*

*pick out their own clothes even if they don't match, and catch lightning bugs past bedtime.* —Age 53

- *Be with my children more and not work nights for twenty-five years.* —Age 63
- *I would have been "all in" for Jesus, sooner.* —Age 29
- *I would love my husband more and not be so serious.* —Age 45
- *Get around big thinkers earlier in life. Invest money sooner.* —Age 49

How would you answer the same question? While you can't get a do-over for the past, you can reinvent your life and live a better future—and a lot can happen in a year!

Remember the Parable of the Fruitless Tree from our last chapter? The vineyard owner came seeking fruit (fruit is the goal) and he found none (that's a big gap). When it comes to the fruit gap between your *ideal* self and your *real* self, how big is the gap between where you are now and where you thought you'd be at this time in your life?

If the fruit is sparse, that's a good reason to reinvent. In order to reinvent in this area, we'll have to drill down a bit more. That means we need to start with a specific, honest, sometimes brutal assessment of the quality and quantity of fruit in our lives—spirit, soul, and body.

How's your fruit? Are you seeing bushel baskets or is it sparse?

## spirit, soul, and body

When we talk about *spirit*, *soul*, and *body*, these may be new concepts, so let's take a moment to define our terms. According to this verse of Scripture, we are a three-part being:

> Now, may the God of peace and harmony set you apart, making you completely holy. And may your entire being—**spirit, soul, and body**—be kept completely flawless in the appearing of our Lord Jesus, the Anointed One. (1 Thessalonians 5:23 TPT)

Understanding our threefold nature will be very helpful when it comes to reinventing areas of our lives. The Bible defines our spirit, soul, and body this way:

**Spirit:** The Bible describes your spirit as the real you. I sometimes explain it this way: Your spirit is the person behind your eyeballs! It's the real you. Your spirit is the person no one but God really knows. God's Word also calls your spirit "the hidden man of the heart" or the "inner man." We might say "the spiritual you." Through your spirit and with the help of the Holy Spirit, you connect with God—the Father of spirits (1 Corinthians 2:11; 1 Peter 3:4; Ephesians 3:16; Proverbs 20:27; Hebrews 12:9).

**Soul:** The Bible describes your soul as your mind, emotions, and will—sometimes we call this our "personality," or our identity. Your soul expresses itself through how you think, feel, and choose. Your soul is located within your spirit (your heart and the real you), and through your soul, you interact with the world around you intellectually and emotionally (Hebrews 4:12; Psalm 23:3; Psalm 103:1).

**Body:** The Bible describes your body as the natural part of you that houses your spirit and your soul. Your body has five physical senses (taste, touch, sight, hearing, and smell). Through your body, your spirit and soul are expressed and interact with the natural world (James 2:26; 2 Corinthians 5:6–8; 1 Corinthians 15:38–44; 1 Corinthians 6:20).

Can you see the distinctions? Of course, these three parts of

our being are integrated and intersect in ways that are often hard to divide—in fact, the only thing that can divide between soul and spirit is God's living Word (Hebrews 4:12).

A simple metaphor for identifying the condition of our spirit, soul, and body is to see them as fuel gauges.

spirit, soul, and body gauges

How's your spiritual life gauge? Running on fumes? What about your soul gauge? Less than half a tank? What about your body gauge? Full tank?

It's good to occasionally evaluate each gauge to locate where you are in relation to where you want to be. When it comes to effectively reinventing our lives, we need to look at our gauges and we need to inspect our fruit.

## fruit inspection

When we inspect our fruit, we'll see the gaps between our *ideal* and *real* self in our spirit, soul, and body. It can be a painful but necessary process. Are you ready? Let's inspect.

## spirit gaps

We'll start with your spiritual health and fruitfulness.

**Your relationship with God.** How's your relationship with the Lord? Do you *know* about God's love, or have you *experienced* it for yourself? What's the distance between your theoretical view of God and your actual experience with Him? (This is a biggie. Because it's so foundational to everything God wants to do in reinventing our lives, we will take a deeper look at this in another chapter.)

**Your spiritual growth.** *Ideal* you is spiritually minded, loaded with the fruit of the Spirit, living by the Word, and praying heaven down, right? You walk with God like Abraham, worship like David, are bold like Peter, pray like Anna, are full of the Spirit like Paul, and close to the Lord like John. *Ideal* you is humble, knows who you are in Christ, loves life, and serves joyfully. But what about the *real* you? Not so much? No worries, you can reinvent!

**Your discipleship.** As the *ideal* you, you're a disciple following Jesus daily, living a God-pleasing, self-controlled, sacrificial life—not to mention guarding your words, loving others, leading people to Jesus, being sold out to the cause of Christ, building His church, and putting a dent in eternity. Uh, but the *real* you needs to wash your mouth out with soap, doesn't like people, forgets to talk about Jesus, and only makes it to church about once a ~~month~~ . . . year.

(I told you the fruit inspection is brutal. Hang in there!)

## soul gaps

This is where a lot of your life is lived—in your mind, emotions, and choices. Your soul affects every area of your life—

relationships, family, finances, vocation, and more. So, let's talk about a few soul gaps.

**Family.** In your *ideal* life, if you're married, what does your marriage and family look like? Enjoying a marriage made in heaven? Kids are nice, polite, and obedient. The rest of the "blood, step, and in-law" gang are great—no issues? Or, in your *real* life is it more like hell on earth and are your family relationships too dysfunctional to describe? (Or somewhere in between?) A God-touched reinvention is possible.

**Relationally.** How are your relationships? *Ideally* you have good relationships—with friends, coworkers, neighbors, and classmates; it's as if you've never met a stranger. But in your *real* life, is it drama central—with narcissism, bitterness, and gossip keeping a steady stream of people coming and going (mostly going)? Thankfully, God will help you create a reinvention roadmap for your relationships.

**Mentally.** How's your thought life? *Ideally* you want peace, joy, clarity, and freedom but in *reality* you struggle with anxiety, fear, confusion, and addiction? Have childhood traumas surfaced and left an ache in your heart and confusion in your mind? Are you struggling to cope? With God's help, you can reinvent, bridge the gap, and find peace of mind.

**Emotionally.** Is there a gap between your *ideal* and *real* emotional self? Living a roller-coaster life? Up and down between happy and sad? Caring and harsh? Positive and negative? Codependent and detached? Selfless and selfish? How's your self-awareness in these areas? (Probably coming into focus as we go through this exercise! *Wink.*) When we allow Him to do so, God does great restoration work in our soul.

**Financially.** When you envision the *ideal* condition of your finances, investments, debt, and generosity, how does it look?

Making the big bucks, completely debt-free, living within your means, investing in high-return funds, tithing, and generously giving away your wealth to all sorts of worthy causes—all while floating on a raft in your infinity pool? Or do words like *always broke*, *never have enough*, *in debt up to my eyeballs*, *practically bankrupt*, and *cheap, tight,* and *stingy* describe your *real* financial life? With God's reinvention ingredients, you'll be able to create the secret sauce you need to close the gap in your financial world.

**Vocationally.** When you consider your calling and how it's lived out in your career, vocation, schedule, and choices, what does the gap between your *ideal* and *real* self look like? Your life purpose filled? Your business flourishing? Your career taking off? Your ministry soaring? Or unfulfilled? Lacking purpose? Bouncing from job to job? Struggling to succeed? Again, God has a reinvention game plan to help here.

(Keep going, this inspection is almost over. Your God-touched reinvention is on the horizon!)

## body gaps

How did *ideal* you expect to look and feel at this time in your life? How does *real* you stack up? Is your *ideal* self a ten, but your *real* self is closer to a three? Have no fear—you can re-invent, close the gap, and no one will recognize you at your next class reunion!

**Health.** How's *ideal* you and *real* you? Have the doctors given you a diagnosis that is causing concern? Doing what you can to eat right, sleep well, reduce stress, strengthen your immune system, and optimize the body God gave you?

Until a few years ago, I had not paid much attention to my body gap. I have never been an exercise person and because I am tall and have had a high metabolism most of my life, I got away with eating whatever I wanted, doing very little exercise, and living life with my foot on the gas pedal—until my thyroid, and one of my parathyroid glands, went kaput!

When my *ideal* self was confronted with my *real* self—and when high levels of blood calcium and thyroid cancer surfaced at the same time—it got my attention!

Thankfully it was not life-threatening, but it was a wake-up call to get with it. I got serious about a new way of eating that works for me, of working out, and of rearranging my schedule. These days, my husband and I are mutually committed to a physical reinvention while we also exercise our faith in His Word. The Lord has promised, "With long life I will satisfy you" (Psalm 91), so we're tapping into His wisdom to reinvent and close the gap.

**Energy.** Are you the Energizer Bunny or basically exhausted? Is *ideal* you kicking it every day, while *real* you struggles to get off the couch? No problem. God will help you charge your batteries with His wisdom.

**Appearance.** Are you comfortable in your own skin? Struggling with body image issues? How big is the gap between *ideal* you and *real* you? God knows your body type and the best way to help you optimize it. And hey, no shame in "painting the barn" as they say. I'm not throwing any stones if you opt for injections, fillers, whiteners, implants, waxing, curling, straightening, micro-needling, or being wrapped up in seaweed. Whatever it takes to help a sister or bro out!

Okay, that's enough. Whew . . . assessing is rough. While it's a difficult process, we have to have a realistic read on the fruitfulness of our lives in order to make changes.

We all have gaps, so don't beat yourself up for yours. They are what they are, but by God's grace you can dig around your roots and fertilize—the Lord will help you reinvent to bring forth more fruit!

## a lot can happen in one year

Now for the most encouraging part of the Parable of the Fruitless Tree—the timeline! While you may have felt fruitless over the past three—or thirty—years, with God's reinventing help you can begin to see big changes in *one year*!

> Sir, let it alone **this year** also, until I dig around it and fertilize it. (Luke 13:8)

One year. I love that Jesus references a timeline in this parable—a lot can happen in one year! Think about how encouraging that is. If you focused on reinventing one or two areas where you see a fruit gap, what do you believe God could do in your life over the next year? Could you be closer to the Lord and strong in faith? Could you be more physically fit? More in control of your thought life and emotions? Warmer and more likeable to those around you? In a better place financially? More successful and closer to realizing your dreams?

The answer is: Yes!

Throughout the rest of the book, we'll talk about many ways to dig around and fertilize your roots. As you listen to the Lord customize each chapter for you, I am confident you'll get all the ingredients you need to fertilize and reinvent your life in these areas. After this fruit inspection, you may feel as if you want to

reinvent *every* area of your life, but as you get started, why not focus on just *one* or *two* areas where you really want to see more fruit—and trust in God's wisdom to dig, fertilize, and reinvent over this next year?

Think about some of these well-known people. While they may or may not be followers of Jesus, there was that *one year* in their journey when things changed for them and the rest is history:

At age 23, Tina Fey was working at a YMCA.
At age 23, Oprah was fired from her first reporting job.
At age 24, Stephen King was working as a janitor and living in a trailer.
At age 27, Vincent van Gogh failed as a missionary and decided to go to art school.
At age 28, J. K. Rowling was a suicidal single parent living on welfare.
At age 28, Wayne Coyne (from the Flaming Lips) was a fry cook.
At age 30, Harrison Ford was a carpenter.
At age 30, Martha Stewart was a stockbroker.
At age 37, Ang Lee was a stay-at-home dad working odd jobs.
At age 38, Stan Lee released his first big comic.
At age 41, Samuel L. Jackson got his first movie role.
At age 42, Alan Rickman gave up his graphic design career to pursue acting.
At age 49, Julia Child released her first cookbook.
At age 52, Morgan Freeman landed his first MAJOR movie role.
At age 57, Kathryn Bigelow finally reached international success, when she made *The Hurt Locker*.

At age 71, Louise Bourgeois was first featured in the Museum of Modern Art.

At age 78, Grandma Moses began her painting career.[1]

If there was one year that made a difference in the lives of these people, just think about what your life could look like twelve months from now if you follow God's step-by-step plan for reinvention by digging and fertilizing around your roots!

The writer of Proverbs gives us hope:

Tend an orchard and you'll have fruit to eat.
Serve the Master's interests
and you'll receive honor that's sweet. (Proverbs 27:18 TPT)

This anonymous quote sums up nicely the reinvention potential of a focused 365 days:

If you know me based on who I was a year ago,
you don't know me at all.
My growth game is strong.
Allow me to reintroduce myself.

This is you.

You have all the potential in the world. God wants to help you reinvent and experience lasting fruit—spirit, soul, and body. Remember, a lot can happen in a year!

Why reinvent? Because *the fruit is sparse*. (But not for long!)

## reinvention review

1. How does this idea that *the fruit is sparse* impact your desire to reinvent your life?
2. How would you describe your spirit, soul, and body gauges?
3. What specific gaps between your *real* and *ideal* self are you most interested in closing and what kind of fruit are you most interested in producing?

section 2

# reinvent reason #2: *the crossroads*

## chapter 3

# he sees you at your crossroads

*Listen as* ***Wisdom calls out****! Hear as understanding raises her voice!*

*On the hilltop along the road, she takes her stand* ***at the crossroads****.*

*By the gates at the entrance to the town, on the road leading in, she cries aloud,*

*"I call to you, to all of you! I raise my voice to all people."*

Proverbs 8:1–4 NLT

I'll never forget my first "crossroads" experience—I was five years old and it was Kindergarten Picture Day.

"Are you a boy or a girl?"

Those mocking words coming at me from a six-year-old, redheaded, freckle-faced boy on the way to kindergarten were my rude awakening to encountering a bully. I had skipped to Windermere Park Elementary school wearing my new school clothes and excited for picture day. When those words stabbed my heart, I was crushed. *Whaaat? How could he?*

"I'm a GIRL!" I cried out, tears in my eyes, as I ran away from that little monster.

In his defense, when I look back at my kindergarten picture, it all makes sense. My royal blue turtleneck and suspenders (yes, suspenders!) didn't help my cause. But I think it was my hair that threw this kid off.

No doubt, my one-inch bangs and three inches of forehead were the culprits that explained the mean kid's question. My dad was a barber, so I had a girl's version of a boy's haircut throughout elementary school.

Still, it was a devastating crossroads and the first time I remember my "skip to school" childhood intersecting with a bully. It was my introduction to the notion that reinventing myself was going to be a thing.

*Beth's kindergarten photo (you be the judge!)*

*(Personal childhood collection.)*

In fact, a few short years later, in second grade to be exact, my neighbor Julie came over to play. As we were flipping through photo albums, she saw *my* kindergarten picture and asked, "Who's this?"

"It's my little brother," I told her. "He died." She never questioned it. I never admitted it. (Not saying this is the way to reinvent, but what happens in kindergarten stays in kindergarten.)

Thankfully, things got better... somewhere around my freshman year in college!

Yep, we all face crossroads!

It's very possible you're facing a crossroads more challenging than my kindergarten crossroads of *childhood innocence meets bully* and the need to reinvent my bad hair and fashion faux pas.

In fact, your crossroads may feel more like a roundabout where recurring patterns of self-defeating behavior have you discouraged. Maybe your crossroads looks like a multiroad junction where several unexpected challenges have converged? Perhaps you're at a fork in the road and trying to decide the best route to a satisfied life in the next season?

Identifying your crossroads will serve as a big motivator and is another good reason to reinvent.

## your crossroads

Do any of these sound familiar?

**"Crisis" crossroads.** Are you facing a crisis or a big life change you didn't ask for—the loss of a loved one, a divorce, or a betrayal? Bankruptcy or job loss? No matter what your crisis crossroads looks like, God's got you and He'll guide you.

**"Season change" crossroads.** Recent graduate? Just married? Baby on the way? Moving to a new city? Empty nest staring you

down? Do you find yourself in the second half of your life and wondering, *How do I put a dent in eternity?* Season changes can be daunting—or they can be exciting and full of hope. In either case, they are the perfect time to reinvent your life.

**"Feeling stuck" crossroads.** Maybe you're really bored at work, very frustrated in your marriage, incredibly unfulfilled in life, or totally financially broke. Thought your career would be more satisfying? Been so focused on building your business and raising kids that you forgot to get a life along the way? You are in the perfect position for a massive, life-changing reinvention to get unstuck!

**"Ticking clock" crossroads.** Hearing the tick of *You're too young* or the tock of *You're not getting any younger*? Tired of the tormenting voices: "You're still single. You haven't had that baby yet. You still live with Mom and Dad"? Also known as being at the "hope deferred" crossroads—your heart is sick because your dreams have not yet materialized, and the clock is ticking. Don't panic—the Lord will help you take practical steps to reinvent your life.

**"Check the baggage" crossroads.** Tired of the same old, same old baggage? Ready to kick an addiction once and for all, end a toxic relationship, get past self-destructive patterns, and release your baggage? It's time to say goodbye to the abuse, manipulation, and codependency! God has a plan for helping you leave the past to live in your reinvented future.

**"Faith matters" crossroads.** Maybe you're a believer or Christian leader and you need a personal revival in your faith life. Maybe you've pulled the *hope levers* and pushed the *prayer buttons*, but the results are frustrating. Struggling to believe? Don't know what you don't know? Perhaps you've been wandering in the wilderness for what seems like forty years. Reinvention in this area is God's specialty.

**"What the..." crossroads.** Are you wondering, *What the heck is going on in our world?* Copernicus-level shifts are happening right before our eyes. No joke. Massive, global changes are taking place in every sector of culture—technology, government, politics, religion, business, media, education, arts, family, and medicine. Old paradigms and operating systems are being vaporized by innovation and rapidly changing values. Then throw in the 24/7 pull of social media and information overload! When you try to keep up, does it feel overwhelming?

If you're at the "What the..." crossroads, it just means there are endless opportunities to leverage the times and trust in the Lord to be creative, innovative, and reinventive!

Of all of the crossroads listed, which ones resonate with you?

Maybe this is the first time you've thought about or identified your crossroads. Or perhaps you've been at your crossroads and ready to reset, reboot, and reinvent for a while, but you haven't known how to move forward? You've prayed, fasted, believed, confessed, dipped yourself in anointing oil, plopped twenty bucks in the offering—even volunteered to serve the two-year-olds in the church nursery—and still, something isn't clicking.

No worries. You are on the reinvention road now and the Lord is going to guide you. While idling at your crossroads, you may be able to hear God's voice, as if He's saying, "Recalculating, recalculating, recalculating, recalculating..."

## recalculating, recalculating, recalculating

Have you ever been on a trip and following the trusty voice of your navigation system only to find yourself at a crossroads you didn't plan on? Perhaps you missed an exit, took a wrong

turn, ended up on a detour...or somehow hot *off* the trail you thought you were supposed to be on.

That's when your maps app starts to chant, "Recalculating, recalculating, recalculating!" Have you ever noticed your nav system *doesn't* say, "You big dummy! That's it. I've had it with you. Why don't you follow my guidance? I'm done. Just figure it out yourself"?

No, your guidance system, in its kind Australian accent (or whatever voice you've selected!), simply says, "Recalculating, recalculating, recalculating," and gives you a new set of directions. This rerouting may make your trip longer than you had planned, but eventually, through a reinvented route, you do reach your destination!

The Lord has a way of doing the same for us. When we face crossroads (good or bad) that require us to reinvent, He's there to guide us—and thankfully, if we end up on a detour we didn't plan on or we inadvertently take the wrong exit, He never says, "You big dummy!" He is full of grace to recalculate our route and get us to His desired destination for our lives.

There is a lot of comfort in that!

Why reinvent? One simple reason: *He sees you at your crossroads.* No matter what crossroads you're at, it's the perfect time to reinvent! With God's help and a few "recalculating" instructions, you can start fresh and love life!

Let's pause for a moment. In these first few chapters, have you already identified the gaps in your life that need reinventing? Perhaps you see yourself at various crossroads and you're inspired to reinvent? That's great! Taking our time in these chapters is important and knowing your reasons to reinvent will give you extra motivation to do so! With that little pep talk, let's look at a few more reasons to reinvent!

## reinvention review

1. In what ways does the reality that *He sees you at your crossroads* motivate you to reinvent?
2. How would you describe the crossroads you're facing?
3. What do you think will happen if you don't reinvent and you remain at your crossroads?

# chapter 4

# he sees your bigger picture

*You've got a new story to write and it looks nothing like your past.*

Anonymous

My mom and I pulled into the Kroger parking lot and there was an awkward silence. She turned to my eight-year-old self and said, "Beth, I need to tell you something. It's not working out with your dad and I... Things just aren't working out... so, we're going to get a divorce."

I froze. Time stood still. I stared at my mom. Then I watched the windshield wipers flip the rain back and forth. I didn't know what to say. Internally, I screamed, *No!!! You can't do this!* After a few minutes of silence, we just got out of the car and went grocery shopping.

I knew in that moment my life had just changed. It was an unexpected crossroads.

What I didn't know is that this crossroads would be the beginning of a reinvented faith journey for me and my family. Turns out it would lead to the biggest reinvention of my life.

Let me share a bit of my journey with you, because there is a good chance you've experienced some type of unexpected,

life-changing crossroads in your life, too. God knows every detail of your story and I want to encourage you. If God could reinvent my life (and our broken family), I have no doubt He will do the same for you.

He sees your bigger picture and perhaps you're on the threshold of the biggest reinvention of *your* life? I hope my story touches yours in some way.

## we were a good catholic family

I was raised Roman Catholic. I loved it all. The stained glass. The crucifix. The incense. I am very grateful for my upbringing. I learned to revere God and gained a basic understanding of God the Father, God the Son, and God the Holy Spirit. Saint Gerard's Catholic Church was a place of awe, wooden pews, and familiar smells. I took my first confession, first Communion, and confirmation name, Theresa, very seriously.

I was in awe of an Almighty God. And I was afraid to die.

As a seven-year-old, I distinctly remember talking about eternity with my little sister, Rhonda. (She was all of six years old!) We tried to get to the end of eternity. We'd talk about a million years. Then we'd add a million more, then a billion more, then a thousand more, then a trillion more—of course, we couldn't get to the end of eternity. As a little kid, I wondered about it—where *did* we go forever? Were we still "alive" after we died? Would I cease to exist?

I didn't know. I asked my parents, and they didn't know either.

And what seven-year-old needs to think about death and afterlife, anyway? (Just go play hopscotch, will ya!)

My life was pretty idyllic. My parents were good people. They were high school sweethearts and married in their early

twenties. They were both funny, attractive, and always the life of any party. Our childhood in Lansing, Michigan, was Norman Rockwell perfect. Mom stayed home with us girls and Dad opened up a neighborhood barber shop. We snow skied on the winter weekends and went up north to our cottage during summer weekends.

Life was great until it wasn't.

### and then there was the divorce

Back to Kroger's parking lot... Everything changed the day my mom told me things were not working out with her and my dad. I was eight years old when my dad moved out, and over the next five years, my parents were separated, then got back together, then separated, and then were finally divorced.

From the day my dad moved out, I felt responsible to step in to help my mom raise my three younger sisters, Rhonda, Kelly, and Michelle—ages seven, five, and four, respectively, at the time. (As if I had any clue on how to "raise" anyone!)

My third-grader instincts kicked in and I called a meeting with my sisters in the basement. Just like a thirty-year-old, I told them, "Okay, you guys, because Mom and Dad are getting a divorce, everyone's going to expect us to be druggies and drop-outs, but we're not going to do it. We are going to be good kids and we're going to get good grades. Okay?"

Meeting adjourned.

My sisters and I survived and actually, in many ways, thrived. I don't know how they did it, but in light of a very difficult situation and their own personal pain, my parents did their best to shield us girls. I'm grateful they didn't bad-mouth each other in front of us.

I remember one piece of guidance my mom gave us after the divorce: "You girls can use this divorce as an excuse for bad behavior *one* time..." That meant we could play the "poor me" card once, but after that we'd be responsible for the choices we made. What great advice that turned out to be. It instilled within us this idea that no matter what happens in life, we can't play the victim card, but rather had to "figure it out" (i.e., we could reinvent!).

When my parents divorced, we stopped going to church as a family. I still wanted to go, so I tried to catch rides with my friends and in junior high, I walked to church by myself—a four-mile round-trip trek! (Yep. You could do that back then.) I was hungry for God but didn't know how to find Him.

And I was still afraid to die.

Let me share what happened next, because you, too, may have grown up "sort of" going to church (or not at all) and may have the same types of fears and questions I had. Perhaps you, too, wonder about life after death and where you will spend eternity.

Jesus answered my questions, relieved my fears, and reinvented my life. I know He's looking to do the same for you, too—no matter where you are in your faith journey!

## freshman year in college

I sailed through junior and senior high school. A good girl. A party girl. A Catholic girl. I embraced my freshman year in college. Still a good girl. Still a party girl. But church fell off the radar at this point.

Andrea, my roommate and childhood friend since our Waverly Winans Elementary school days, challenged my faith. In high

school, she was funny and always stunning. At the end of our senior year, Andrea became "religious."

As it turned out, Andrea came into a relationship with Jesus, and as she and I roomed together during our freshman year of college, I had a front-row seat to her transformation.

I watched. I listened.

I think she was the first person I knew who actually seemed to *know* Jesus.

I didn't ask, but she told me three things the Bible said about a personal relationship with Jesus Christ. Andrea always started off sharing Bible verses by innocently saying something like, "Oh Beth, look right here in the Bible it says..." and then she'd read a Scripture that went right into my heart like a "God-zinger"!

She told me about Matthew 7, and I knew I was on the "broad" way: "You can enter God's Kingdom only through the narrow gate. The highway to hell is broad, and its gate is wide for the many who choose that way. But the gateway to life is very narrow and the road is difficult, and only a few ever find it" (Matthew 7:13–14 NLT).

She told me about Revelation 3, and I knew I was lukewarm: "I know all the things you do, that you are neither hot nor cold. I wish that you were one or the other! But since you are like lukewarm water, neither hot nor cold, I will spit you out of my mouth!" (Revelation 3:15–16 NLT).

She told me more about Matthew 7, and I knew He didn't know me: "Not everyone who calls out to me, 'Lord! Lord!' will enter the Kingdom of Heaven. Only those who actually do the will of my Father in heaven will enter. On judgment day many will say to me, 'Lord! Lord! We prophesied in your name and cast out demons in your name and performed many miracles in your name.' But I will reply, 'I never knew you. Get away from me, you who break God's laws'" (Matthew 7:21–23 NLT).

I had never heard these things before, but the part about life after death had my attention.

If the three Scripture passages Andrea shared with me were true, I was in trouble.

I also caught the part that God was not interested in my religiously lukewarm condition—He wanted more, a personal relationship with me. I remember walking around my college campus thinking about those Scriptures and realizing how much I didn't know about God or life after death.

At nineteen years of age, I was not ready for a God-shift. I had just found my college groove and was enjoying life. I wasn't perfect, but I figured if God graded on a curve, I was probably good enough to slide into heaven with a B– or a C+. (Later I found out God doesn't grade on a curve and my "good enough" life was not going to be "good enough" to get me into heaven. That was slightly alarming.)

During this time, I went to a Bible study with Andrea (I must've looked like a deer in the headlights). I scanned the room and noticed something—cute boys . . . I mean . . . joy? Life? Anyway, after a couple of "hallelujahs," I realized these Bible people definitely had something I did not have, and, honestly, I didn't know if I wanted it.

But one thing was clear: While I knew my religion, they knew their God.

Andrea's pastor gave me a Bible and I secretly started reading it. I was surprised by how "alive" it seemed. It was as if God was talking directly to my heart. I distinctly remember reading the Gospel of John and then I read Romans and Hebrews.

Whoa! I had never heard some of those things.

In all my reading, I was happy to find out how much Jesus said about going to heaven. It was both a relief and problematic. Through reading the Bible, my eyes were opened to several things.

First, Jesus was the truth and the only way to heaven (John 14:6).

Second, I had to be "born-again" to get into the kingdom of God (John 3:1–6).

Third, I was a sinner and needed a Savior (Romans 10:13).

Basically, Jesus was knocking on the door of my heart, and I needed to make a choice. Would I invite Jesus into my life or would I continue to control the steering wheel?

I wrestled with all of this for another six months, because I knew that if I ever did become "born again" (reinvented!), I was going to be *all in*. So, I grappled. *Do I do it now? Wait a few more decades? Hope I don't die in the meantime?* I sensed the Lord persistently and patiently knocking on the door of my heart, night after night.

By the end of my freshman year in college, I came to a point of decision. (Turns out, it's not any fun to live on the fence between the "sinful college life" and "saved Christian life.") I realized Jesus wouldn't barge into my life uninvited, but if I would open my heart and receive Him as the Lord of my life, He would come in.

So, I did, and He did.

I was born again, and my religion turned into a relationship.

My "invitation prayer" wasn't that dramatic. I was sitting at a kitchen table with a few friends and internally making the decision to become a Christian. Finally, I said it out loud to my friends: "Okay, um, today, um, I decide I'm gonna be a Christian!"

That was it. The most "unpolished" salvation prayer ever.

But in that moment, in my heart, I surrendered to Jesus and He became the Lord of my life. I gave Him the steering wheel of my heart. *#jesustookthewheel*

Instantly, I felt His peace. Jesus came in. My heart was happy.

As a new believer, I started to grow in my relationship with

the Lord, albeit without much directed effort on my part—a Bible study here, a church service there. I finally landed in my first spiritual home, the Campus Crusade for Christ at Western Michigan University in Kalamazoo.

Within the next couple of years, the Lord changed, rearranged, and transformed just about every area of my life—whew... there was a lot to reinvent, but I was growing. Knowing Jesus was with me every step of the way gave me indescribable joy and peace; I wanted everyone to know Him.

All in all, this was a sweet season of skipping along with Jesus.

The birds chirped more sweetly.

The sky seemed bluer.

Life was good.

I was saved.

## god sees a big future for you

Back when I was a kindergartener with one-inch bangs, God saw the bigger, eternal picture.

As I sat in the Kroger parking lot with my mom that day, God saw the bigger picture.

He was causing all things to work together for my good. He was working a plan to lead me to Christ and to truly reinvent my eternal life.

I have no doubt; the Lord has done or is doing the same thing for you. He sees a big future for you. He's causing all things—your childhood, your teen years, your adult years—to work together for your good, your eternal good.

Perhaps, in His bigger picture, He's orchestrated the fact that you're reading or listening to this book, right now. (God has a way of doing those types of things!) Either way, He *is*

orchestrating your ultimate, eternal reinvention and if you've never surrendered to Christ, today is a good day to become a born-again Christ follower.

When you think about your story and the big future God has for you, your most important reinvention event of all, as it is for everyone, is being born again.

The lasting and eternal success of all the fun reinventions we're going to talk about in this book is directly connected to your personal relationship with Jesus, so if you've never confessed Jesus as your Lord, how would you like to pray the same "unpolished" prayer I did?

If you know you need a Savior and are ready to surrender your life to Jesus, feel free to use the same words I did: "Okay, um, today, um, I decide I'm going to be a Christian!" Amen!

He heard you!

Now you can spend the rest of your life growing as a Christian and getting to know Him—He's wonderful and He has a great plan for the rest of your life!

And for those of you who have been born-again Christians for many years, this is the perfect time to recommit your life and future to the Lord. Not only does He have an eternal home for you in heaven, but He also has big plans for you on earth. Acknowledging His Lordship in your life is a good way to let Him know you're still all in!

You can pray a heartfelt, "unpolished" prayer, too: "Father, today I recommit my life to Christ. I want to know You better and I just want You to know I am all in!" Amen!

There's nothing better than knowing the Lord and walking with Him into your future destiny!

Why reinvent? Because *He sees your bigger picture.*

## reinvention review

1. When you think about the idea that *God sees your bigger picture*, how does that impact your reinvention?
2. What has your faith journey been like? Can you describe your life *before* coming to know Christ as well as *after* coming to know Him?
3. Revisit your story—how did you come to know Jesus?

section 3

# reinvent reason #3: *the future*

# chapter 5

# you're a hero on a journey

> *We have become his poetry, a re-created people that will fulfill the destiny he has given each of us, for we are joined to Jesus, the Anointed One. Even before we were born, God planned in advance* ***our destiny*** *and the good works we would do to* ***fulfill it****!*
>
> Ephesians 2:10 TPT

No matter what you think of Tiger Woods, you can't argue with his reinvention. Winning his fifth Masters Jacket in 2019 made him only one of two golfers who could claim fifteen major championships. He was on top of the world when he won his first Masters in 1997, but in recent years, he, along with everyone else, wondered if he'd ever again play golf at the competitive level we'd come to expect. Over the past ten years, he's faced numerous crossroads: the public humiliation of a sex scandal, a DUI arrest, multiple knee surgeries, a torn Achilles, and back fusion surgery.

If Tiger was to make a comeback, he would have to reinvent himself. He did.

His Masters win at Augusta in 2019 was a story of reinvention

and redemption, and that brought many of us watching to tears. His was the classic hero's journey—the stuff blockbuster movies and best-selling novels are made of.[1]

You may be more like Tiger Woods than you realize! No matter your victories or setbacks, as you seek God's purpose for your life, He's got a hero's journey with your name on it.

## you could be a hero

Why reinvent? Because your future is bright and you could be a hero! The Master (*wink!*) has put plans, purposes, and gifts within you. You were born for such a time as this, and this is your time to get with it!

Maybe you think, *Who me?* Yes, you!

God is in the business of raising up unassuming, world-changing visionary types.

When you think about Bible heroes who have made a mark, why couldn't you become a leader like Gideon or Esther? Advance women's rights like the Daughters of Zelophehad? (Who? Check them out—they are the bomb! *#girlgang*) Be a world-changer like Abraham, Moses, or David? You could put a gospel dent in eternity like Peter, Paul, and Mary (the Bible ones).

And who says you can't represent the Lord like some of our modern Christian heroes? Billy Graham, Mother Teresa, or Tim Tebow, selfless legends that they are?

Somebody has to be the next Steve Jobs. Why not you? Why couldn't you be one of the Sharks (of the *Shark Tank* type—okay, so you're not a billionaire... but still)? There's no reason you couldn't follow in the reality TV footsteps of Chip and Joanna Gaines, Dog the Bounty Hunter, or Bear Grylls!

Someone is going to invent the next generation of artificial intelligence applications; it could be you or your grandkids. People will still be creating TV series, blockbuster movies, and legendary songs for years to come—imagine you are one of the people doing it!

Any reason you couldn't run a marathon? Go to med school? Figure out how to fund vertical, aeroponic growing systems throughout hunger-stricken parts of the world? Eradicate cancer? Build homes for widows and orphans in third-world countries? Live in outer space, own a driverless automobile, or raise organic monkeys? (We're brainstorming right now and there are no bad ideas . . . ha!)

There are discoveries to be revealed. Cures to be discovered. Systems to be designed. Creative ideas to be developed. Innovations yet to come. There is no reason in the world God couldn't use you to do these things.

Ever heard of Uzziah?

> Uzziah was sixteen years old when he became king, and he reigned in Jerusalem fifty-two years. His mother was Jecoliah from Jerusalem. He did what was pleasing in the LORD's sight, just as his father, Amaziah, had done. Uzziah sought God during the days of Zechariah, who taught him to fear God. And **as long as the king sought guidance from the LORD, God gave him success.** (2 Chronicles 26:3–5 NLT)

Uzziah was a king (at sixteen!). He was also a developer (vs. 6), a builder (vss. 9–10), an agricultural and civil engineer (vs. 10), a military hero (vss. 6–9, 11–15), and an inventor (vss. 14–15)! He engineered the early catapult to launch rocks and protect his city. As long as he sought the Lord, God made him prosper. His was

the perfect hero story (until he quit seeking the Lord and pride became his downfall).

Heroes, stay humble.

The Bible is loaded with heroes who've saved, invented, designed, and discovered things. Of course, Jesus is the ultimate hero, but God also delights in transforming our lives for His greater purposes.

Embrace it—another great reason to reinvent is because the Lord has an incredible plan for your life and you're a hero on a journey!

## everyday heroes

As a fresh college grad, I once worked for a hero! The renowned sports medicine physician and orthopedic surgeon Dr. Lanny Johnson. He was writing surgical textbooks for medical students and I was the faithful transcriber of his dictated tapes.

As a Christian, Dr. Johnson believed, with God's power, he could change the medical world, and he did!

He is known for being a pioneer in the development of arthroscopic surgical procedures for the knee, shoulder, elbow, and hip. He influenced hundreds of orthopedic surgeons and helped athletes in nearly every sport. Dr. Johnson is the inventor of the motorized instrumentation still used worldwide today in all such arthroscopic surgical procedures and he invented the first nonreactive bio-absorbable implants for orthopedic surgery. He's highly regarded as a dedicated innovator, teacher, and entrepreneur.

When I worked for Dr. Johnson in 1981, surgeons from all over the world flew to his medical lab in East Lansing, Michigan, to watch and learn as he performed arthroscopic surgery. He never

failed to tell them they were witnessing medical surgery done in the power of the Holy Spirit. He was a bold Christian, committed to the Lord and dedicated to discovery in medicine.

As a result, he gave the Lord credit for revealing countless methods and innovations to him. Dr. Johnson has been granted over seventy-five U.S. patents for his discovery and invention in medicine, surgical procedures, surgical instruments, and various sports equipment.[2]

In addition to his work in medicine, Dr. Johnson was an excellent Bible teacher and offered a Wednesday Bible study at the end of the workday for anyone who wanted to attend. His vibrant and practical faith teachings were loaded with life-changing revelations that continue to impact me decades later.

At eighty-six years of age, he's still discovering and inventing new things! (He recently received another new patent approval!) He wrote on his blog (yes, he blogs!), "I want to make it clear, I am not retired. Retirement is bad for one's health. I concluded my clinical practice in 1995 but work regularly in various endeavors. I do not see anywhere in the Bible where retirement is to be desired or realized. I have told my daughters that I will not be speaking at my retirement party."[3]

I knew Dr. Johnson was a big deal when I worked for him, but I was too immature to recognize the "hero status" he really had. Reading his curriculum vitae will expand your vision and faith!

His blog article titled "Life and life" is an example of what I mean. He wrote:

> These are musings about Life and life. Notice the capital letter on the first Life. The reason is that it is a synonym or code name for the person of Jesus Christ of Nazareth. He called himself the Way, the Truth, and the Life. Over the

years I have lived an imperfect life (not capitalized) which is one of the qualifications for becoming and remaining a Christian. There is a fun scripture that rhetorically says, "Does a well man need a doctor?" Only those with faults need apply.[4]

I hope you're inspired by Dr. Johnson's journey. How might the Lord use you to discover, invent, or reinvent?

Let me tell you about another hero.

We were recently at the celebration-of-life service for a very successful and generous Christian businessman we'd come to admire. He'd owned several companies over his life, and while not a perfect man, he tried to live in a way that honored the Lord.

As a boy, because of the generous sponsorship of a woman he didn't know, he was able to attend a Christian summer camp where he gave his life to the Lord and was hugely impacted. Later in life, as he gained success in his businesses, he decided to pay it forward for other kids.

For several decades, he anonymously gave a part of his wealth to sponsor over 5,000 kids so they could attend a Christian summer camp and come to know Christ.

You probably wouldn't know his name, but heaven does.

He put a dent in eternity for thousands of others.

I think he's a hero in heaven.

What about you? Is your vision for life expanding? What "heroic" kinds of things does God want to do in and through your life?

## blockbusters and bestsellers

Speaking of heroes, I've always been impressed with anyone who writes fiction! To read a page-turning novel is a fun escape from the stress of real life and stirs up a fresh bit of creativity.

A few years ago, the desire to write a novel began to germinate within me. (I'm still a long way from doing it, but the desire is growing!) I'm a Bible teacher, so it's easy for me to think in a "line-upon-line" way to explain a biblical truth or revelation—whether through writing or speaking. But to write fiction? It's so intimidating!

I had no idea how to write a novel until a friend set up a meeting for me to meet *New York Times* bestselling author Patti Callahan Henry. She was gracious and welcomed my husband and me to her home to visit and so I could ask a few questions about writing fiction. She introduced me to the "character arc" and the "hero's journey" and gave me several great recommendations for learning more.

Although I was nodding as if I understood her description of these things, in truth, I was trying to wrap my head around the ingredients to writing good fiction. I'm still learning how to reinvent my own writing in this way, but at least now I can identify the hero's journey or character arc being played out in blockbuster movies and bestselling novels.

With that disclaimer, in very general terms—from a nonfiction writer, with my rookie understanding—let's talk about how your reinvention hero's journey might look!

your hero's journey

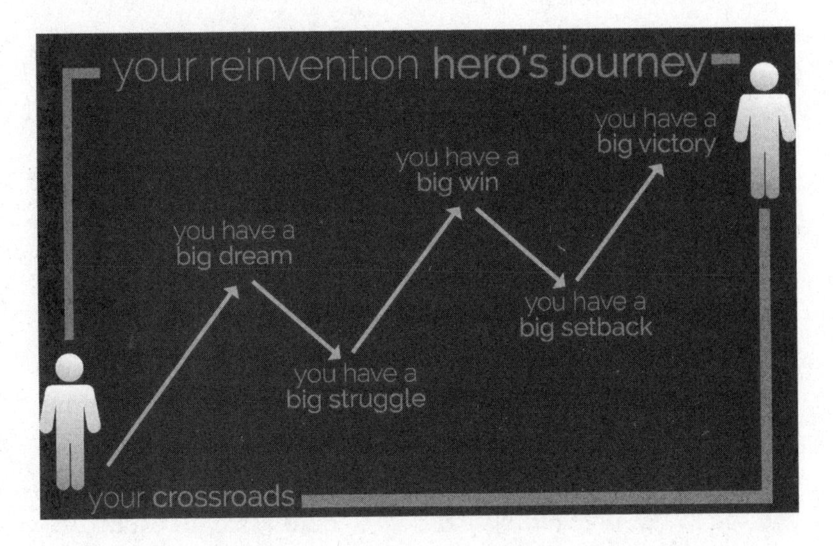


*Once upon a time...*

**Your crossroads.** You're minding your own business and then—*boom*—you face a crossroads. It could be like any of the crossroads we've discussed—exciting, like moving to a new city or having your first baby, or challenging, like a divorce or the loss of a job. Your crossroads serves as an "inciting incident" and your reinvention journey begins. A hero's response to any crossroads is to dream big...

**You have a big dream.** You have a lofty dream and a strong desire to overcome any challenge and reach your God-given potential. You want to live a big, purpose-filled life, find success, help others, and put a dent in eternity! This is more than a whim. You want this bad, and your dream won't take no for an answer.

**You have a big struggle.** The problem is, you try to reach your dream in your own strength and you have a hard time realizing your goals. You struggle with internal insecurities and external difficulties. Two steps forward and three steps

backward, it seems. You finally reach the end of yourself and seek help—from the Lord and the family, friends, and mentors He's put in your life.

**You have a big win.** You follow the wisdom of your mentors and the leading of the Holy Spirit. By employing your assets—your gifts, talents, resources, and experiences—things start to work! You have a big win. Everything you touch seems to turn to gold. Your dream is coming into focus. Life is great!

**You have a big setback.** Everything is going according to plan—until it isn't! Whatever could go wrong does! Your dream is fading; your hopes are dashed. Storms and valleys take their toll. You are at your lowest point and on the verge of quitting. Things that are supposed to work out, don't. Doors that are supposed to open, close. People who are supposed to be with you betray you. Your own foolish choices have cost you more than you wanted to pay. Your hopes have been deferred and you feel heartsick. Everything takes so long! These setbacks make you second-guess everything. You're less self-assured and yet more dependent on the Lord.

**You have a big victory.** If your dream is going to come to pass, it's now or never. You dig deep to revisit your God-given calling, your eternal purpose, and your internal motivation. Externally, you face bigger giants but internally, you are more certain that with God all things are possible. It's time to take big faith steps and go for it! You do. You win. Your dream has come to pass! Jackpot! Everyone shouts, "Hallelujah!" Roll the credits.

**Your reinvention.** You started fresh and now you're loving life! *And they all lived happily ever after.*

On paper or in a film, the hero's journey is a fun thing to behold! One thing is for sure—when the character arc or the

hero's journey is strong, that story is a winner! (And of course, this is what God does in your life as you reinvent!)

What phase are you at in your hero's journey?

In real life, the hero's journey is exhilarating and challenging, but worth every scene. He has a bright future with a happy ending ahead for you! The good news is that you're not on the hero's journey alone—when you acknowledge Him, He'll guide you every step of the way.

> Trust in the LORD with all your heart,
> And lean not on your own understanding;
> In all your ways acknowledge Him,
> And He shall direct your paths. (Proverbs 3:5–6)

## the hero's journey in a poem

I remember a particular season in my journey and the encouragement God gave me, which inspired me to write a poem.

It was a cold, snowy February afternoon in 1982, and as I looked out the back window at my mother's house, I couldn't help but notice how bland her winterized pool and pruned rosebushes looked. I thought back to how gorgeous her sparkling blue pool and rose-laden bushes looked in the peak of summer, and I was struck by the contrast I saw in the dead of winter.

Words began forming in my heart as the Lord gave me this poem about the seasonal reinvention of a hero: "The Rosebush."

***The Rosebush***

*The rosebush is the queen of flowers in the summer when she blooms,*
*but when the leaves are changing colors it's her turn to be pruned.*

*The bush that once was marveled at and praised for all her splendor*
*is cut right down—to the ground, a stub with no one to tend her.*

*Through winds and rains and blizzards of snow her bark is still the same.*
*She really feels like a failure now and begins to take the blame.*

*She doesn't like the way she looks, so short, so bare, so dead,*
*she wonders if she'll bloom again the way the Handbook said.*

*But as the snow begins to melt and the Son shines on her branches,*
*she feels the growth well up within and she does a few rose dances.*

*Fuller, more beautiful, more fruitful she grows,*
*but what it took to get her there only she and her Maker know.*

Ever felt like that rosebush? Little did I know then how much the hero's journey of the rosebush would encourage me through many seasons of reinvention. I hope it encourages you, too.

He wants to turn your *once upon a time* into a *happily ever after*.

Why reinvent? Because your story is not over and *you're a hero on a journey*!

## reinvention review

1. When you think about being *a hero on a journey*, how does that impact your expectation to reinvent?
2. What phase are you at in your own character arc or hero's journey?
3. Can you relate to the rosebush? If so, what season are you in?

# chapter 6

# you're the best fixer-upper on the block

*Did someone say "Shiplap"?*

*Fixer Upper*

I'm slightly obsessed with Chip and Joanna Gaines of *Fixer Upper* fame. And so are millions of other people. What do we love about them? She's the gorgeous, introverted design genius. He's the outgoing life of the party. They're real. Normal. Funny. They live their faith. They have a cute family.

They've reinvented shiplap!

In 2013, Chip and Joanna rediscovered shiplap, a design element found in old farmhouses, and reinvented its use for accent walls, kitchen backsplash, fireplace mantel walls, kitchen islands, ceiling inlays, and more.

By 2016, it was the design trend of the year! Not only have they brought shiplap back, by pouring their heart and soul into fixing up the worst house in the neighborhood, but they've also put the art of reinventing homes on the map![1]

Just like Chip and Jo reimagine forgotten aesthetics or turn broken-down buildings into sparkling dream homes, the Lord does no less with you and me.

Ever felt like a beat-up and dilapidated old house? God has

a renovation in store for you! Why reinvent? You're the best fixer-upper on the block and He's ready to flip you—as long as you're up for a reinvention!

## feel like a fixer-upper?

After college, I was in a funk and having heartfelt conversations with the Lord: "Father, help! Here I am with a college degree and I feel Your call to the ministry—but I don't even know what that means. I'm trying to sort out Your will for my life. I am waiting on tables at the Harrison Roadhouse tavern...and not living the dream. Lord, I need a breakthrough!"

I was as sincere as I knew to be. I was not looking for a spiritual "magic wand" to transform my life—well, mainly because I knew it didn't exist—but I truly wanted a lasting breakthrough and His direction for my life.

Around this time, I moved Michelle, one of my best friends, to Jacksonville, Florida, for her new job. As we drove from Michigan through the mountains of Kentucky and Tennessee on the way to Florida, I took note of the partly cloudy, partly sunny day as I drove up and down the mountains and valleys.

I was praying a "breakthrough" prayer (again!) when the Holy Spirit gave me a little song and His insight:

Partly cloudy,
partly sunny,
some days are like that,
isn't it funny?

He continued reassuring my heart with these thoughts: *You're driving to Florida under the clouds, through the valleys and*

*mountains—a metaphor for your experience as a Christian—but you will be flying home on a jet above the clouds where the skies are blue. That's where I'm taking you spiritually.*

After we got to Florida and my friend was settled in, I continued seeking the Lord for a breakthrough! One afternoon, as we walked into a Wendy's restaurant for lunch, the Holy Spirit spoke to my heart: "Be ye transformed!"

I knew it was the Lord and I found it funny. "God? You're talking to me in a Wendy's?"

I felt His Spirit quickening my heart and as I walked up to the counter to order, I responded to the Lord internally: *Yes, Lord, that's what I want! Transformation! Breakthrough! Yes! Be ye transformed? How?*

"By the renewing of your mind," I sensed Him telling me.

I knew my Bible enough to know He was quoting Romans 12.

> And do not be conformed to this world, but **be transformed by the renewing of your mind**, that you may prove what is that good and acceptable and perfect will of God. (Romans 12:2)

But still I asked, "How, Lord? How do I renew my mind?"

Michelle and I ate our lunch and went back to her house to continue unpacking. As I pondered all of these things, I didn't realize it, but I had just entered a *Romans 12 Fixer-Upper* season.

That same night, we decided to visit a small church to find Michelle some new friends. We'd never been to this church before, and it was obvious we were "the visitors."

At the end of the service, the pastor called my friend and me up to the front and shared a word he felt the Lord had given

him. I had not experienced this type of thing before, but I was sincerely seeking the Lord for a breakthrough and sensed His presence, so up to the front we went.

The pastor, Bob, looked at me and said, "For you, it's been partly cloudy and partly sunny..." (Whoa, did he just say those exact words?) He went on to say the Lord would give me clarity for my life.

I was speechless.

This pastor had no way of knowing anything about my prayer time with the Lord or the song He'd given me. It was very encouraging to say the least!

After the service, Pastor Bob met with me and my friend, and he gave me two teaching series on cassette tape. (For those who wonder what a cassette tape is, it was how we listened to music *before* Spotify, iTunes, MP3s, CDs, and they came just *after* albums, 8-tracks, and Morse code!) You'll never guess the name of one of the teaching series he gave me: "Renewing the Mind"—again, I was stunned.

God was up to something!

That encounter rocked my world in the best way. Every day for the next two weeks I lugged my cassette player, lots of batteries, and those cassette tapes to my lounge chair on Jacksonville Beach. I listened to those tapes over and over, and God went to work reinventing my life by renewing my mind to His Word and who I was in Christ.

As a result, I began to see myself the way He saw me—in Christ! The more I listened to those messages, the more God renewed my mind and transformed my life with His vision for my future.

When I returned home from Florida at the end of those two weeks, it wasn't "partly cloudy, partly sunny" any longer! I did fly home in a jet above the clouds where the skies are blue, but

it wasn't just a natural flight home—there had been a spiritual breakthrough and I flew home as a different person.

Perhaps you can relate to some or all of the above! Maybe things have been "partly cloudy, partly sunny" and you, too, have been asking the Lord for a breakthrough?

Let me share what He shared with me. I know it will encourage you.

## be transformed: reinvention realities

> **Be transformed** by the renewing of your mind. (Romans 12:2)

When the Holy Spirit spoke the words *be ye transformed* to my heart as I walked into Wendy's, what did that mean? *Transformed* is from the Greek word *metamorphoo*, from which we get the word *metamorphosis*.[2]

You remember the process of a caterpillar turning into a butterfly, right?

In the chrysalis, the caterpillar, with its very limited beauty, mobility, and long-term prognosis, goes through a metamorphosis and is transformed into a gorgeous butterfly with unlimited mobility and a bright future! (Sounds like a reinvention to me.) Of course, we've all seen this transformation process and it's dramatic!

Do you know your transformation can be *as* dramatic as what happens when a caterpillar becomes a butterfly?

Have you ever mistaken a caterpillar for a butterfly? Of course not. Why? Because they don't look anything alike! The process of transformation does that. In the same way, God will take areas of your life that are very "caterpillar-ish" (and where there

are big gaps!) and through His transformational work He will reinvent your life to the point where you don't look anything like your previous self.

How does this metamorphosis work? For us and the caterpillar?

For the caterpillar, while inside the chrysalis, it actually digests itself and turns into a gooey substance.

Caterpillar soup!

In that soupy condition, all of its structures are reinvented and reorganized. (Crazy, eh?) A metamorphosis takes place. The transformation is so substantial that what started as a caterpillar emerges as a butterfly.

Thankfully, *you* don't have to digest yourself into a soup.

But in areas where you are caterpillar-ish, if you will allow God's process of transformation to take place within you, He'll go to work reorganizing, restructuring, and reinventing things on the inside of you. Then, in due season, you'll come out ready to fly—and looking nothing like your old self!

How does the Lord do this? How does He transform, reorganize, restructure, and reinvent our lives?

Simple: through the renewing of our minds!

## renewing the mind: reinvention strategy

> Be transformed by the **renewing of your mind**. (Romans 12:2)

Did you know "to renew your mind" literally means "to renovate your mind"?[3]

God wants us to experience transformation (reinvention) by the renewing (renovating) of our minds! Often, when we think

of a renovation project, we think *demolition*. Knocking down walls, ripping out cupboards, and removing all of the old things, and then installing new wall treatments, flooring, fixtures, and decor. Again, Chip and Joanna Gaines are the masters! They love a good "demo day"!

However, when it comes to renewing and renovating our minds, we have an advantage. We don't have to spend much time on the demolition. Jesus took care of that for us!

> This means that anyone who belongs to Christ has become a new person. **The old life is gone**; a new life has begun! (2 Corinthians 5:17 NLT)

Our job is to spend time installing the new—renewing our minds to who we are in Christ! The more we renovate our minds with God's Word, the more we'll effortlessly and "automatically" experience transformation and reinvention.

For example, as you read, believe and say what God's Word says about you—you're renovating your mind. You're *installing* new truths, new attitudes, new beliefs, and a new operating system—and you are being transformed.

The more you renovate your mind with God's Word, the greater the transformation.

### renovate with paint

This is how the Lord explained it to me.

Picture it like this. Your mind represents the walls of a room in your fixer-upper house. God's Word represents buckets of paint with all the colors you need to transform your room.

To renovate your mind and experience transformation, you

need to paint the walls with the new colors of God's Word. But how?

Open up your Bible (the buckets of paint) and search for scriptural truths and promises (colors) that belong to you in Christ! Once you identify one or more truths, you renovate (paint) the walls of your mind by believing and speaking God's words over your life—not as a mantra or positive-vibes type of thing, but actually from your heart, as something you truly believe. The more you believe and speak His Word, the more coats of paint you put on the walls of your mind. After a period of time, you'll notice the walls of your mind have been completely renewed and renovated and—voilà—you have been transformed!

For example, let's say the walls of your mind are covered with the *dark red* paint of discouragement and depression, but you'd really like them to be the *bright white* color of joy and favor!

Rather than continuing to paint the walls of your mind with *dark red* paint by thinking, believing, and saying things like, "I'm so depressed. Nothing goes my way. I never get a break. Why does everyone else have it so great?" you remove the lid from your bucket of paint (i.e., crack open your Bible) and find the colors you desire. That is, you find His promises for new *bright white* walls!

You paint that *bright white* color onto the walls of your mind by believing and saying what His Word says. As you believe and say these kinds of things, you'll be renovating your mind:

"I rejoice in the Lord always" (Philippians 4:4).
"I will praise the Lord" (Psalm 34:1).
"If God is for me, who can be against me?" (Romans 8:31).
"God's favor surrounds me" (Psalm 5:12).

"The joy of the Lord is my strength" (Nehemiah 8:10).
"I'm His Beloved" (Romans 8:16).
"I'm blessed coming and going" (Deuteronomy 28:6).

What will happen? When you inspect your renovation, you'll see the *dark red* walls of your mind are no longer *dark red*, but a slight transformation has occurred and now they are *dark pink*.

You're making progress, but this is no time to quit painting!

One coat of paint did not renovate the room. Your mind is not fully renewed, so keep on painting! Dip your paintbrush into God's Word again; believe and speak: "He is making a way where there is no way" (Isaiah 43:16); "God is giving me His wisdom" (James 1:5); "My path is growing brighter and brighter!" (Proverbs 4:18); "In Jesus's name!" The walls of your mind are no longer *dark red*, nor *dark pink*. Now they're *light pink*!

You may wonder, how will you know when to stop painting—how will you know when your transformation is complete?

You'll know when *it is*—and until you *know*, just keep painting!

Continue putting up coats of your bright white paint by declaring, "I reign in life through Jesus Christ" (Romans 5:17); "He orders my steps" (Psalm 37:23); "I am more than a conqueror through Christ" (Romans 8:37); and pretty soon, those *dark red* walls turn *dark pink*, turn *light pink*, and finally, after dozens of coats of paint, transform into the *bright white* walls you desire.

Your mind has been renovated and you *are* transformed!

You don't have to try to *not have* dark red walls, because now you actually *do have* bright white walls! You aren't "trying" to be transformed; you "are" transformed!

This is reinvention! It's time to bring in the furniture and start living.

What type of reinvention transformation do you need in your

"house"? What color are the walls of your mind right now? What promises (colors) has God given you in His Word (buckets of paint)? Begin to renovate the walls of your mind with the paint of God's Word by believing and speaking it over your life.

This is God's supernatural fixer-upper process of transformation!

Why reinvent? It's simple—because God has a bright future ahead for you and *you're the best fixer-upper on the block.*

Are you catching it? So far, we've covered three big reasons to reinvent: the gaps, the crossroads, and the future. I hope you are seeing the importance of taking time to process these things and evaluate your starting point. This will be helpful when we begin to develop your reinvention roadmap in the second half of the book. If you're getting antsy for the reinvention how-tos, hold tight—we need to look at just one more significant reason for reinventing: the love. You're gonna love this!

## reinvention review

1. How does knowing *you're the best fixer-upper on the block* inspire you to reinvent your life?
2. When you think about God's power to transform the "caterpillar-ish" parts of your life into a beautiful butterfly, in what areas do you desire that change?
3. To experience the transformation you desire, what Scriptures can you use to renovate (paint) your mind? List them.

section 4

# reinvent reason #4: *the love*

# chapter 7

# it's his love, not yours

*If God had a refrigerator, your picture would be on it. If He had a wallet, your photo would be in it. He sends you flowers every spring and a sunrise every morning... Face it, friend. He is crazy about you!*

Max Lucado

"Love is a many splendored thing," the Four Aces said. Whitney Houston promised, "I will always love you." Elvis Presley admitted he "can't help falling in love." The Beatles said, "All you need is love," but Air Supply is "all out of love." Queen wanted "somebody to love," but Justin Bieber leaves it open: "as long as you love me." At least Foreigner was honest when they admitted "I want to know what love is."

Love is the dominant theme of thousands of songs.

We are wired for love; we want to be loved and we want to love—yet, why does the experience of love elude so many? Why is it we often feel unloved, rejected, disapproved of, shamed, isolated, alone, and unaccepted? Why do we put up walls, withhold love, and spin around in self-defeating patterns?

We have a love gap and we need a massive reinvention in this area!

This is so basic and yet so important. Succeeding in all of the reinvention how-tos we are going to discuss in the second half of the book won't give you the deep satisfaction you are seeking if you are not established in God's love. Let's zero in to explore God's love—I guarantee it will revolutionize your life and give you the strongest foundation possible upon which to reinvent!

## the love gap

While we need and deeply desire the love of our parents, our family, our spouse, and our friends, it's not just human love we need—our spirit (our innermost being) desperately craves and needs God's love. After all, at our core, we are spirit beings and God is the Father of spirits.

When we have a real, deep-calls-to-deep type of love relationship with God from His spirit to our spirit, nothing can match that type of love.

No matter how many humans love you, the love gap is present when you have not *experienced* God's love—practically for yourself.

Can you relate to the love gap?

Maybe you *know* God loves you, but you're not *experiencing* His love to the degree that you'd like. Or maybe you've drifted from the Lord and feel God is mad at or disappointed with you, and you wonder, "Does God still love me?"

God wants to reinvent your life in this area!

The apostle Paul prayed an incredible prayer, that you too can pray, to *experience* the reality of God's love:

> May Christ through your faith [actually] dwell (settle down, abide, make His permanent home) in your hearts! May you be rooted deep in love and founded securely on love,
>
> That you may have the power and be strong to apprehend and grasp with all the saints [God's devoted people, the experience of that love] what is the breadth and length and height and depth [of it];
>
> **[That you may really come] to know [practically, through experience for yourselves] the love of Christ, which far surpasses mere knowledge [without experience]**; that you may be filled [through all your being] unto all the fullness of God [may have the richest measure of the divine Presence, and become a body wholly filled and flooded with God Himself]! (Ephesians 3:17–19 AMPC)

### my story of the love gap

I can tell you from personal experience, when the Lord answers this prayer and fills the love gap in your life, it is the game-changing mother-of-all reinventions!

God never intended for His love to be theoretical.

He went to extreme measures to demonstrate His love to you through Jesus Christ—and He wants you to experience it, practically, for yourself!

Allow me to share a bit of my experience with the life-changing revelation of His love. What God did for me I know He wants to do for you!

Years ago, I hit a gusher!

You see, I had been a born-again Christian for many years prior to the gusher. Jesus was the Lord of my life and I knew

God loved me; I had experienced His love in *doses* throughout my Christian life, but then . . . the *gusher*!

Let me take you back . . .

As a brand-new Christian, I began to grow in my faith and while I knew the Lord was with me, I kept making mistakes and had perfected how to live "the defeated, roller-coaster Christian life"!

I was bouncing back and forth between faith and feelings.

One day I felt close to the Lord and the next day I felt discouraged. One day I felt like a Christian and the next day I felt I wasn't measuring up with my attitudes, words, and behaviors. I spent half of my Bible-reading and prayer devotion time with God confessing my sins and telling the Lord I was sorry for a host of failures.

I was struggling with the *experience* of God's unconditional love. And the thing is, I *wasn't* living a rebellious, backslidden life—I was actually doing my best to live a life pleasing to the Lord.

I needed a gusher.

While I *knew* the Lord loved me in my head, I longed for the *experience* of His love in my heart.

Now, the truth is, on the outside, you wouldn't have known I struggled with the experience of God's love within my heart, because generally, I am a glass-half-full type of person. I was usually happy and content—yet, deep down there was this dull sense of rejection.

It wasn't until later in life I understood that the internal feelings of rejection and abandonment and what some call the "orphan's spirit" were likely connected to my parents' divorce back when I was just a kid. (Not complaining. I always felt, with the knowledge they had at the time, my parents did the best job they could have done raising us kids. Still, a spirit of rejection tried to pop up from time to time.)

In my *head*, I *knew* He loved me and I was grateful. Yet, in my *heart*, I still desired to *experience* His love. (Who's with me?) I had prayed the prayer in Ephesians 3 many, many times over the years—perhaps hundreds of times.

And then, one day, the gusher!

Here's what happened...

## it's his love for you, not your love for him

For me, the gusher—the *experience* of God's love—came not through a goose bump or a euphoric feeling but through a *revelation* of His Word.

The Lord opened up 1 John 4:10 to my heart in a way I had never seen:

> This is real love—**not that we loved God, but that he loved us**. (1 John 4:10 NLT)

Wait, what? I read it again: *This is real love—**not** that we loved God, but that He loved us.* It's NOT that we loved God? But I thought it was.

Wait—it's that He loved us?!

It was a flip-the-script moment!

This basic truth is the bedrock for your lasting reinvention. Without this revelation, your reinvention efforts, no matter how successful, will feel empty. That's why experiencing God's love is a huge reason to reinvent.

All of my Christian life I had done my best to love the Lord, to love my family, to serve Him, to pray, to worship, to teach, to write, to help people, and to co-pastor with my husband—*because* I loved the Lord.

That wasn't a bad thing, but that wasn't THE THING!

It's NOT that I loved God; it's that He loved me! That meant God's love for me *wasn't* contingent on my performance, my works, my checklists, my good deeds, my strivings, or my noble life and ministry pursuits. (And it turns out, that's an exhausting way to live the Christian life!) Of course, I knew this in theory, but when the script was flipped, it hit me in a fresh way.

Again, when I thought about my framework for life—my obedience, my prayer life, and my favorite worship songs—it was all about *my* love for the Lord, not His love for me. (Anybody else relate?)

My favorite songs were "I Love You Lord" and "My Jesus, I Love Thee," and at that time, I couldn't think of a single song about *God's love* for me, other than the children's song "Jesus Loves Me." (Thankfully, the revelation of God's love is flowing throughout the world these days and many more songs about His love have come forth!)

Now, I would've told you all of my "efforts" to love and please the Lord *weren't* intended to garner God's favor. But when I thought about it, my ability to receive from the Lord was more about what *I had to do* (obey God, release my faith, love my enemies, live a holy life, speak His Word, serve people with gladness, and a host of other things) and less about what *He had done* for me.

And the truth is, unconsciously I sort of felt God "owed" me His blessings since I was "doing" the right things. (Don't throw stones.) After all, I had been pulling the faith-levers, pushing the "possess the land" buttons, and avoiding the "big sins" for years, so of course God was obligated to bless me. (Insert self-righteous wink.)

Obviously, I never verbalized this, but it was apparent when

my hopes were deferred: That's when I got a little perturbed with the Lord. Why wasn't He coming through for me?

What was taking so long? What was *I* doing wrong?

When I discovered the simplicity of receiving "every good and perfect gift" from Him *not* because I loved Him, but simply *because* He loved me, it was too good to be true!

In the same way I could not do one thing to earn or qualify for my salvation, except to believe and receive Jesus, I could not do anything to earn or qualify for the benefits of His salvation, including the experience of His love.

My job? Believe and receive.

His job? Everything else.

This basic revelation turned on the lights and rang the bells—jackpot! He loves me!

Are the "God loves you" revelation lights turning on for you, too? If not, keep reading. (Actually, keep reading either way!)

### it's not just knowing; it's believing

As I continued reading in 1 John 4, this verse lit up like a Christmas tree: "And we have **known and believed the love** that God has for us" (1 John 4:16).

Yes, I had *known* about God's love for many years, but I'm not sure I actually *believed* it. Perhaps I doubted it. During this *love gusher* reinvention, I decided to actually, on purpose, *believe* the love God had for me.

At. All. Times.

When things went my way and when things didn't go my way, I chose *to know and believe* the love God had for me and I was confident His love was at work on my behalf.

It's so simple. So basic. So life-changing!

While I had *known* God loved me most of my Christian life, the gusher experience of His love started flowing when I *believed* it!

It was my choice.

I know *and* believe the love God has for me because it's not that I loved Him; it's that He loved me!

The more I pondered these thoughts, the more I actually *experienced* the breadth and length and height and depth of God's love, practically, for myself. The more I experienced His love, the less I strived and the more I relaxed and rested in His love.

The less I focused on *my love for the Lord*, the more I experienced *His love for me*. God's love was no longer the greatest-sounding *ideal* theory I'd ever heard; it was *real*.

Now, don't get me wrong; I *still* loved the Lord, loved people, worshipped, prayed, gave, served, and did my best to obey Him and follow the Spirit's leading, but now all of my "deeds" were a *response* to His love, not a *condition* for receiving it.

Can you see the difference? Do you relate to all or parts of my story?

I sincerely hope you are sensing the joy, freedom, and rest that comes from the gusher of His love! If you've heard or *known* God loves you, let me encourage you to "believe it!"

Go ahead and flip the switch of faith and believe the love God has for you.

When you *experience* God's love, it will be a spiritual reinvention of epic proportions—you'll never be the same. The revelation of God's love is your foundation for a massive reinvention!

Why reinvent? Because there is a whole new world waiting for you when you realize *it's His love—not yours.*

## reinvention review

1. How does the revelation that *it's His love, not yours,* flip the script for you when it comes to reinventing your life?
2. Have you experienced the "love gap" in your own relationship with the Lord?
3. How would you describe the difference between "knowing" and "experiencing" God's love in your life?

## chapter 8

# it's better than you thought

*The love of Jesus is the love you and I have been looking for all of our lives.*

Timothy Keller

John was a writer and a runner; he loved to fish and was a bit of a handyman.

But the thing I like the most about John is that he had a revelation of God's love. It was easy to tell. It was the way he spoke and the way he wrote. And there was this phrase he used. In one of his books, he used this phrase five times and that was the tipoff—"the disciple Jesus loved."

Of course, I'm talking about the apostle John. He wrote five books of the Bible, he outran Peter on the way to the empty tomb (only a guy would put that detail in the story!), he was a fisherman, he repaired the nets, and he knew Jesus loved him (John 20:2–9; Matthew 4:19–21; John 13:23).

John had a revelation of God's love.

Listen to how John explained it in 1 John 4, from the Passion Translation of the Bible:

**This is love: He loved us long before we loved him. It was his love, not ours.** He proved it by sending his Son to be the pleasing sacrificial offering to take away our sins.

Delightfully loved ones, if he loved us with such tremendous love, then "loving one another" should be our way of life! No one has ever gazed upon the fullness of God's splendor. But if we love one another, God makes his permanent home in us, and we make our permanent home in him, and his love is brought to its full expression in us. And he has given us his Spirit within us so that we can have the assurance that he lives in us and that we live in him.

Moreover, we have seen with our own eyes and can testify to the truth that Father God has sent his Son to be the Savior of the world. Those who give thanks that Jesus is the Son of God live in God, and God lives in them. **We have come into an intimate experience with God's love, and we trust in the love he has for us.**

**God is love!** Those who are living in love are living in God, and God lives through them. **By living in God, love has been brought to its full expression in us so that we may fearlessly face the day of judgment, because all that Jesus now is, so are we in this world.** Love never brings fear, for fear is always related to punishment. But love's perfection drives the fear of punishment far from our hearts. Whoever walks constantly afraid of punishment has not reached love's perfection. **Our love for others is our grateful response to the love God first demonstrated to us.** (1 John 4:10–19 TPT)

Let's go just a bit deeper on this topic. When it comes to reinventing your life, I can't think of any single truth that

will give "stickiness" to your reinvention than the revelation of God's love.

It's better than we thought!

## it's the "because-then," not the "if-then"

When it comes to experiencing God's love, understanding the huge difference between the "if-then" Christian life versus the "because-then" Christian life is a significant game changer.

**If-then.** The "if-then" life goes like this: *If* I do things like obey the Lord, make sacrifices, and walk in love (all good things), *then* He will bless my life. The "if-then" life is about what I do to qualify for God's blessings.

**Because-then.** The "because-then" life goes like this: *Because* of what Jesus did through His obedience, sacrifice, and death on the cross, *then* I can believe and receive the benefit of His love and goodness. The "because-then" life is more about what Jesus has done through His finished *work on the cross* than what I do through my *works in the flesh*.

This is another way of saying, "It's not that we love the Lord, but that He loves us!"

I love the way Timothy Keller, founder of Redeemer Presbyterian Church in New York City, put it in a recent tweet: "Religion makes us proud of what we have done. The gospel makes us proud of what Jesus has done" (@timkellernyc).

No wonder the psalmist said, "Your lovingkindness is better than life" (Psalm 63:3). The result of receiving this revelation is that we *will* have a heartfelt desire to obey, sacrifice, and love the Lord and others—as an overflow response to His love, not as a condition for receiving it.

Now, if all of this isn't enough, there's more! Let me share one more tidbit.

## god loves you just as he loves jesus

On the practical side, how does God love you? How big is His love? He loves you just *as* He loves Jesus!

> Love has been perfected among us in this: that we may have boldness in the day of judgment; because **as He is, so are we in this world**. (1 John 4:17)

Look at that little phrase: "as He is, so are we in this world." I always assumed this passage meant we could have boldness in the day of judgment, *if* we are as loving and kind in this world as Jesus is (a lot of "if-then" performance in that!).

But the whole context of 1 John 4 is about God's love, not our works. He's telling us that we can have boldness in the day of judgment because as Jesus is *loved* (beloved) in this world, so are we! In other words, the context of this verse is, "As Jesus is loved, so are we in this world."

Remember? It's not that we loved God; it's that He loved us!

Again, the emphasis is on what *He did* to demonstrate His love for us, not on what *we do* to demonstrate our love for Him.

Can you see that? Because you're a Christian and "in Christ," your Father loves you just as He loves Jesus! Let that soak into your spirit—it's so liberating!

Need more?

Read what Jesus said about God's love for us:

> I do not pray for these alone, but also for those who will believe in Me through their word.... that the world may know that You have sent Me, and **have loved them as You have loved Me**. (John 17:20, 23)

Jesus wants us to know the Father "loves us just *as* He loved Jesus." But, how much *does* He love Jesus?

> And suddenly a voice came from heaven, saying, **"This is My beloved Son, in whom I am well pleased."** (Matthew 3:17)

The Father called Jesus His "beloved"—His "dearly loved" (NLT)—in whom He was well-pleased. This was said *before* Jesus did anything! Before the miracles, before He walked on water, before He multiplied bread and fish, before He blessed kids, and before Jesus went to the cross...the Father was well-pleased with His beloved Jesus—unrelated to His performance!

This is great news, because He loves you *just as He loved Jesus*!

Are you catching this?

I hope you are experiencing a great sense of relief and rest as this truth of how loved you are registers in your heart!

Your Father calls you His beloved and He is well-pleased with you—*before* you do anything! (Let me say it again louder for those in the back: *Your Father calls you His beloved and He is well-pleased with you—before you do anything!!*)

This passage in Romans summarizes it beautifully:

> And you did not receive the "spirit of religious duty," leading you back into the fear of never being good enough. But you have received the "Spirit of full acceptance," enfolding you into the family of God. And you will never feel orphaned, for as he rises up within us, our spirits join him

> in saying the words of tender affection, "Beloved Father!" For the Holy Spirit makes God's fatherhood real to us as he whispers into our innermost being, **"You are God's beloved child!"** (Romans 8:15–16 TPT)

Let's put an exclamation point on this chapter by looking at how science confirms the benefits of a healthy foundation in God's love. Dr. Timothy Jennings, author of *The God-Shaped Brain*, said:

> Does it matter which God-concept we hold to? Recent brain research by Dr. Newberg at the University of Pennsylvania has documented that all forms of contemplative meditation were associated with positive brain changes—but the greatest improvements occurred when participants meditated specifically on a God of love. Such meditation was associated with growth in the prefrontal cortex (the part of the brain right behind our forehead where we reason, make judgments and experience Godlike love) and subsequent increased capacity for empathy, sympathy, compassion and altruism. But here's the most astonishing part. Not only does other-centered love increase when we worship a God of love, but sharp thinking and memory improve as well. **In other words, worshiping a God of love actually stimulates the brain to heal and grow.**[1]

I hope these two chapters on God's love have stirred up something deep within you. I know the Lord wants you to experience the breadth and length and height and depth of His love practically for yourself.

When you experience God's love for yourself, you'll *want* to reinvent your life in a way that is pleasing to Him. His love gives you confidence that you really can start fresh and love life!

Why reinvent? Because His love *is better than you thought*!

We've spent the first half of the book helping you to unpack the 4 Reasons to Reinvent Your Life—the Gaps, the Crossroads, the Future, and the Love.

With this strong foundation, you are now poised to successfully reinvent your life—spirit, soul, and body! That means you have every reason to reinvent and every opportunity to reach your potential in your relationship with the Lord, your family, and others; in your mental and emotional health; in your entrepreneurial and ministry endeavors; and in your physical health and wellness!

So, buckle up and let's shift gears as we talk about the practical *how-tos*! How will you reinvent? That's going to be our focus for the rest of the book as we answer the 4 Questions to Reinvent Your Life.

## reinvention review

1. How does the idea that God's love *is better than you thought* help you in the reinvention process?
2. When you think about the "if-then" and the "because-then" ways of seeing God and His love for you, what does that do for you?
3. Have you ever thought about your Heavenly Father loving you "just as" He loves Jesus? What does that mean to you?

part 2: love life!

# 4 questions to reinvent your life

## chapter 9

# meet the maven

*If you do what you've always done, you'll get what you've always gotten.*

Tony Robbins

I'll bet by now you're ready to begin customizing your reinvention roadmap and creating your own reinvention secret sauce. Well, it's finally time to dig into the practical reinvent how-tos embedded in an easily overlooked story in the Bible.

Let's meet the Maven.

How did a grieving, widowed single mom of two boys, who was being hounded by her creditors, reinvent her life and end up as a successful, entrepreneurial oil tycoon? This remarkable woman—whom we affectionately call the Maven—answered the 4 Questions to Reinvent Your Life found hidden in her story in 2 Kings 4.

Reinvent Question #1: *What do you want?*
Reinvent Question #2: *What do you have?*
Reinvent Question #3: *What will you do?*
Reinvent Question #4: *Why will you do it?*

Answering these questions was the key to a God-touched reinvention in her personal life, in her family, and in her finances.

Together, in our remaining chapters, I will help you answer these four questions as you develop your own step-by-step reinvention game plan.

So, without further ado, let me introduce you to the Maven and the four reinvention questions veiled in her story:

> A certain woman of the wives of the sons of the prophets cried out to Elisha, saying, "Your servant my husband is dead, and you know that your servant feared the LORD. And the creditor is coming to take my two sons to be his slaves."
>
> So Elisha said to her, "**What shall I do for you?** Tell me, **what do you have in the house?**" And she said, "Your maidservant has nothing in the house but a jar of oil."
>
> Then he said, "**Go, borrow** vessels from everywhere, from all your neighbors—empty vessels; do not gather just a few. And when you have come in, you shall shut the door behind you and your sons; then **pour** it into all those vessels, and set aside the full ones."
>
> So she went from him and shut the door behind her and her sons, who brought the vessels to her; and she poured it out. Now it came to pass, when the vessels were full, that she said to her son, "Bring me another vessel."
>
> And he said to her, "There is not another vessel." So the oil ceased. Then she came and told the man of God. And he said, "Go, **sell** the oil and **pay your debt**; and you and your sons **live on the rest**." (2 Kings 4:1–7)

Let's rehash her story.

Up until she found herself at this reinvention turning point, this woman and her husband, Mr. Prophet-in-Training, had been loving life, raising their two boys, and serving God. Somewhere along the way, they got into debt. Maybe her husband was unable to make ends meet? Perhaps they had borrowed a few shekels—to renovate their house or to invest in a business?

We don't know how they got into debt, but we do know that suddenly her husband passed away and real life kicked in with a vengeance. No sooner had she left her husband's funeral than the creditors were banging on the door seeking their funds. Worse, if she didn't pay up, they were threatening to take the two most precious things she had left—her two sons—to be their slaves! (And it's likely, if she didn't pay her debts, she'd end up a slave as well.)

No doubt about it, she had all the *reasons to reinvent*!

You can imagine her temptation to be fearful and angry. The *gap* was real. This *crossroads* flipped her script and it didn't seem fair. Her *future* looked bleak. Maybe in her *ideal* world she saw herself married to the keynote speaker of the annual prophet's conference, living in her cute house with a white picket fence and loving on the two cutest boys in all of Israel. But in her *real* life, things had just come crashing down—her husband was dead and the creditors were coming to take her boys.

What were her choices—surrender to their fate as slaves or find the strength to transform her situation?

She needed to reinvent—and fast! And the good news? She did!

In this heartbreaking situation, she sought God's help by going to the godly person positioned to coach her—the prophet Elisha. She reminded him of her husband's reverence for the Lord and his faithful service. This was no minor matter. History

with God counts for something, and their service to the Lord had not gone unnoticed.

In response to the Maven's desperate cry for help, because of His *love*, the Lord answered her, but not with a big bag of shekels to pay off the loan or a hit of Tinker Bell dust that would make all of her problems go away—instead, through Elisha, as she answered the four reinvention questions, she received God's sequential, systematic, step-by-step reinvention game plan.

The result? She had supersonic success, paid her debts, kept her sons, and loved life!

She modeled a holistic, faith-filled, God-touched reinvention that propelled her life forward—spirit, soul, and body!

The Maven, who started out as a desperate, indebted, grieving, widowed single mom of two boys, found the mother lode of God's reinvention strategy and was transformed into a successful, faith-filled, confident, purpose-driven, anointed, entrepreneurial oil tycoon—not to mention a godly woman and loving mother.

That's why I like to call her the Maven! (And in case you've not used that word lately, by definition a *maven* is a man or woman who is *dazzlingly skilled in any field*. Synonymous with being a hotshot, superstar, virtuoso, whiz, sensation, star, ace, champion, and expert.)[1]

She blazed a reinvention trail for us to follow.

Helping you answer the 4 Questions to Reinvent Your Life will be our focus for the rest of the book. In each chapter, I'll highlight the Maven's story and the pertinent biblical narrative—and all the while I'll share practical and inspirational insights, stories, and innovative secrets to help you reinvent areas of your life.

This will be your chance to gather the wisdom you need

and to prayerfully connect the dots to create your own unique, strategic reinvention roadmap.

To get the most out of each chapter, I encourage you to continue highlighting and writing down the revelation God speaks to your heart and be sure to take time for self-reflection in the Reinvention Review at the end of each chapter.

You ready? Let's answer the *4 Questions to Reinvent Your Life!*

## reinvention review

1. In what ways does *meeting the Maven* inspire you to reinvent your life? In what ways do you relate to her?
2. At first glance, which of the four reinvention questions interests or intrigues you the most?
3. Are you ready to trust the Holy Spirit to help you as you spend focused time reading the remaining chapters, answering the four reinvent questions, and writing your own step-by-step reinvention roadmap?

section 5

# reinvent question #1: *what do you want?*

## chapter 10

# it's okay to want what you want

*Sometimes I just want someone to hug me and say, "I know it's hard. You're going to be okay. Here's a coffee. And 5 million dollars."*

Anonymous

I'll never forget the day I lost my daughter Annie. True story.

I was grocery shopping with all four of our kids in a large grocery store. (Slight lapse of judgment there. The kids were three, five, seven, and nine years of age at the time.) My cart was loaded with groceries and as I approached the checkout counter and began unloading, I did the usual child-count…Meghan, *Annie*, Luke, Eric—where was Annie? Annie was seven years old and our second born. I asked the three other kids if they knew where Annie was. But all I got back were blank stares.

My head felt like it was on a swivel as I ran up and down the checkout area shouting at the top of my lungs, "Annie! Annie! Annie!"

I didn't see her anywhere.

I looked at the cashier with a glare that said, "Shut down the store! We have a lost child!" I didn't care how ridiculous I looked or sounded—I *wanted* to find Annie!

Panicked, I continued shouting louder, "Annie! Annie! Annie!" Nothing. I told the other three kids to hop on the cart and I pushed that loaded cart back toward the grocery aisles at a speed I didn't know was possible and went up and down them shouting, "Annie! Annie! Annie!"

Finally, I heard a whimper in the cereal aisle. There she was!

Incredibly relieved, I snatched her up and gave her a suffocating bear hug…and told her to never leave us again. What a relief it was to find her!

But let me tell you what I *didn't* do.

I didn't get to the checkout counter, notice Annie was missing, ask the other kids if they'd seen her, and then shrug my shoulders and say, "Oh well, I have three of my four kids. Sure, it would be nice to go home with all four of them, but three is a majority. Better luck next time…"

Never! Are you kidding me?

I WANTED to find Annie and we were not leaving that store until we found her, and I left with ALL four kids! (If you've ever lost a child in a store, you know the feeling.) My *want* fueled all my behavior in that incident.

There is something about a heartfelt *want* that will propel you toward your desired end.

So, let's talk about it by looking at Reinvent Question #1: What do you want? Over the next several chapters, let me encourage you in these things:

It's Okay to Want What You Want
It's Better to Want What God Wants
Go After a New Bullseye
Go Small and Stay Home
Go Big and Work on Your Magnum Opus

### reinvent question #1: what do you want?

> A certain woman of the wives of the sons of the prophets cried out to Elisha, saying, "Your servant my husband is dead, and you know that your servant feared the LORD. And the creditor is coming to take my two sons to be his slaves."
>
> So Elisha said to her, **"What shall I do for you?"** (2 Kings 4:1–2)

Your reinvention strategy starts with this first question: What do you want? God, through the prophet Elisha, was offering the widow His reinvention help by asking her a simple question: "What do you want?"

It's interesting to note Elisha didn't ask her, "How much do you need? When is your deadline? How did you get into debt? Why don't you have any money saved up?" His first question was, "What shall I do for you?" (i.e., "What do you want?"). Apparently, it was important that she identify, recognize, and verbalize her wants.

So, what *did* she want? She *wanted* her boys!

Sure, she wanted the money she needed to pay the creditors, but a stronger desire was driving her heart: She didn't want to lose her boys! This wasn't a whimsical "Oh, it would be nice to not lose my sons to the creditors . . . you know, I'd hate for them to become slaves . . ." No! She was desperate.

She desperately *wanted* to keep her boys!

What about you? What do you want? When you think about your life—spirit, soul, and body—what are you desperate for? What do you want the Lord to do for you? What are your earnest, heartfelt wants and desires? Know God? Get married? Have kids? Get out of debt? Win your family to Christ? Buy a house? Start a business? Earn your degree? Travel? Lose weight? Be healthy? What do you want?

There is a reoccurring Bible theme related to the importance of identifying our wants, desires, and longings. And you might be surprised: The message is that it's okay to want.

## want what you want

It's okay to want what you want. (Unless, of course, you want to rob a bank, beat people up, sell crack, or some other ungodly thing, but I doubt that's you.)

I have found many believers struggle with the idea of "wanting their wants."

They've been taught to be content with what they have (which is good) and they've been told "God will meet your needs, but not your wants." So, they lower the bar of expectation and settle for less. It's true, He does meet our needs according to His riches in Christ, but the Bible also has a lot to say about our wants and God's desire to fulfill them.

While the Lord wants us to be content with what we have, He also wants us free to experience His goodness and generosity. This gives God pleasure! Let's look at this. Jesus said:

> But seek the kingdom of God, and all these things shall be added to you.
>
> Do not fear, little flock, **for it is your Father's good pleasure to give you the kingdom**. (Luke 12:31–32)

As a parent, you understand this, right? It gives you pleasure to bless your kids. If you're a grandparent, you take great pleasure in spoiling your grands. God feels that way about you. Listen to what Jesus said about the Father's *much more* desire to bless you with good things.

> If you then, being evil, know how to give good gifts to your children, **how much more will your Father who is in heaven give good things** to those who ask Him! (Matthew 7:11)

Your Heavenly Father wants to bless you with good things even *more* than an earthly parent desires to do! (And He likes it when we have a grateful and generous attitude about these things.) Did you ever notice when Jesus performed the miracle of multiplying the fives loaves of bread and the two fish to feed 5,000 men (plus women and children) that they were able to eat "as much as they wanted" (John 6:11)? That's how good God is. (I've found the longer I walk with God, the "gooder" He gets!)

At His core, God is a giver. He is not a withholder:

> For the LORD God is our sun and our shield.
> He gives us grace and glory.
> **The LORD will withhold no good thing**
> from those who do what is right. (Psalm 84:11 NLT)

If you wrestle with the idea that God is a buzzkill and doesn't want you to have anything, let the lovingkindness of your generous "more than enough" Heavenly Father reinvent your view of Him.

The notion that God loves you and wants to be good to you may be new to you.

I understand. I am not in any way trying to minimize the very real struggle you may have in renewing your mind to the truth about God's character, or allowing yourself to want. When you've spent a lifetime suppressing wants and desires, going without, getting leftovers, and fighting for your own survival,

the last things you need are pie-in-the-sky, flowery, religious clichés to help you "reinvent" your life.

If you grew up hearing more about God's desire to limit your happiness or withhold His goodness, it's time to reinvent your view of God. If you were led to believe God was usually mad at you and you missed out on the "God loves you" part, it's time for a new pair of Jesus-glasses.

Now don't get me wrong. God doesn't want us to have an entitled, greedy, or covetous disposition. And it's true that *apart* from Christ, we *were* lost in our sin and separated from God, but when Jesus *is* the Lord of your life, it's time to awaken to the goodness of God and newness of life in Christ.

It's okay to want. Permission granted. He wants you (wait for it) "blessed to be a blessing." Cliché, but true!

So, what do you want? How bad do you want it?

## the difference between a want and a desire

"I want abs, but I need tacos." Anyone else? Okay, but really.

Let's talk about the difference between a *want* and a *desire*. Wants are on the surface; desires go deeper. Desires are the want behind the want!

For example, the Maven *wanted* money to pay her creditors, but her real *desire* was to keep her sons. Both were important—one was deeper. Her *want* was based on desperation, "the creditor is coming." Her *desire* was based on love, a desire to keep her sons so they wouldn't be taken.

You may say, "I want a pay increase. I want more income. I want more money in my life." But the truth is while you might *want* more income, your real *desire* is the freedom more money will bring you. More money will bring you freedom to pay all your

bills, to purchase the things you need, and to enjoy the life you desire. More money will empower you to give generously. More money will give you peace of mind and less stress and worry.

So, while you *want* money, what you really *desire* is the freedom money will give you. Do you see the difference?

Here's why this is important: Desire fuels want.

*Want* is like a car with no gas.

*Desire* puts gas in the car and gets it moving.

For example:

**Want: I want to have a good job.**

**Desire:** I desire to make an eternal difference with my time, so I will only take a job that allows me to serve His cause.

**Want: I want my kids to know the Lord.**

**Desire:** I desire that my kids have a genuine, personal encounter with God, so I will rearrange my schedule and my finances to do whatever it takes to teach them about the Lord, and to get them to church, and to place them around people who will help them know the Lord.

**Want: I want to get my master's degree.**

**Desire:** I desire the knowledge and pay increase that comes with a master's degree, so I will say no to certain things to set aside the next two years to earn my degree.

We all have wants, but desire brings them to pass. Desire won't take no for an answer. That's what Proverbs describes: "Life

motivation comes from the **deep longings of the heart**, and the passion to see them fulfilled urges you onward" (Proverbs 16:26 TPT).

So, the question is: What do you want? More importantly, what do you *desire*?

A story is commonly told of a young boy in the swimming pool with his very successful uncle.

The little boy asked, "Uncle, what does it take to be as successful as you are?"

With that question barely out of his mouth, his uncle pushed him underwater. The boy tried to come up for air and his uncle pushed him a little deeper. The boy was kicking and thrashing around trying to get to the surface when, finally, his uncle grabbed him by the shoulders and pulled him up out of the water so he could catch his breath.

"Sonny," his uncle said, "when you desire to be successful as much as you just desired that last breath, you'll be a success, just like your uncle!"

Well, that's one way to teach a lesson! Thankfully, the Bible teaches us about desire in a less traumatic way.

## be honest about what you want

As you answer the question "What do you want?" this is not the time to be a people pleaser or to suppress your God-given dreams. Dr. Caroline Leaf—cognitive neuroscientist with a PhD in communication pathology and a BSc in logopedics and audiology, specializing in metacognitive and cognitive neuropsychology (aka a boss!)—describes a type of cognitive dissonance (or mental discomfort) that can occur "when you lie to yourself and are not true to who you are."

> When you lie to yourself and are not true to who you are, you can experience an internal "war"—what you say and do is not in agreement with what you are thinking about or what you want. This can impact both your mental and physical health, because a lack of mental congruence drains your energy, causes toxic stress and affects the way information is processed and memory is built, which leads to neurochemical chaos in the brain and body.[1]

Nobody wants to live with chaos in their brain or body, so be honest about what you want—what you really, really want!

The good news is that if you will spend time with the Lord, allowing His Word to dwell in you richly, He will align your desires with His!

Jesus said, "If you abide in Me, and My words abide in you, you will ask what **you desire**, and it shall be done for you" (John 15:7). Literally the words *you desire* mean "the things you desire, the things you will, the things you have in mind and wish. The things you love, take delight in and have pleasure in."[2]

The amazing thing about this verse of Scripture is Jesus *isn't* talking about *His desires* for you—He promises if you stay close to Him and allow His Word to live in you, then you can ask Him for what *you desire*. What I love about this incredible statement from Jesus is He knows when we live in Him and His Word lives big in our hearts, then our wants and desires will be transformed to be in alignment with His will for us. In other words, when you seek Christ in all things, He will work in you to align your wants with His best for your reinvention.

Isn't all of this liberating?

Developing your reinvention strategy begins by answering

Reinvent Question #1: What do you want? The good news is that *it's okay to want what you want*!

## reinvention review

1. In what ways does this chapter and the idea that *it's okay to want what you want* challenge and transform your thinking?
2. When we spend heartfelt time with the Lord and in His Word, what happens to our wants and desires?
3. When you think about your *wants*, what are the deeper *desires* driving what you really want?

## chapter 11

# it's better to want what god wants

*What God knows about us is more important than what others think.*

Tim Tebow, *Shaken: Discovering Your True Identity in the Midst of Life's Storms*

It wasn't too long ago that Amanda, a friend of mine, was reporting directly to the CEO of an influential company in Southwest Michigan where she emceed events, produced podcasts, coordinated conferences, and more to help move this organization forward. This was a prestigious role for a gal in her midtwenties!

As much as Amanda enjoyed her job, she felt something was missing. She asked to meet for coffee and told me, "You know, I just don't feel like I'm doing what I'm supposed to be doing. There's still something in me that's not satisfied. I feel like I'm supposed to do something with more eternal value." She loved the people she worked with and she loved what she was doing, but the "purpose-shaped" hole within her wasn't being filled. She *wanted* to find and fulfill her God-given purpose.

As we talked, we came up with a plan for her to intentionally seek the Lord for His direction over the next thirty days. She

wanted God's will, but rather than waiting for a "feeling" or a billboard to drop from heaven with her answer, I encouraged her to spend some extra time in prayer and reading her Bible and to journal any Scriptures or thoughts the Lord quickened to her heart. I reminded her that God's will is revealed in His Word, so after thirty days, when she reviewed her journal notes, His direction would be crystal clear.

She did exactly what we discussed. The Lord spoke to her through His Word. She told me that the Scripture that had really solidified the direction for her was 1 Timothy 1:12: "I thank Christ Jesus our Lord who has enabled me, because he counted me faithful, putting me into the ministry."

She said, "It was such a word from God to my heart and gave me the confirmation that I wasn't manufacturing this change on my own or making the wrong move—but He was actually putting me into the field of ministry... and He was enabling me to do it!"

When she shared what the Lord had been speaking to her, I responded (half kidding and half serious), "Well you know, we'd love to have you around here, but your salary would basically be cut in half. We need somebody like you! Your experience and skill set would be perfect here to help us get the message of the Bible basics to the world!"

I fully expected her to dismiss the idea because, in all honesty, I thought there was no way she'd take a massive pay cut to fill the role we needed. To my pleasant surprise, she and her husband talked about it and decided she should take the position we had available. It was a big decision, but she left her job, came on staff with us, took a big pay cut, and has done an excellent job. As an executive director on our church leadership team and the executive producer of all things related to *The Basics With Beth* outreach ministry, she is a high-capacity

leader, and she's doing a phenomenal job with our TV program, podcasts, online courses, and more.

Did the Lord honor her decision? Indeed! After she accepted the position, her husband was offered the dream job he wanted, with an increased salary!

She said, "We haven't even felt the effects of the pay cut." She went on to say, "I work just as hard here as I did in my previous job, but I'm so much more fulfilled because I know I'm doing something that is affecting eternity."

I've asked her, "Do you have any regrets?"

"Not one," she said.

Two years after she came on board I asked her, "Now that you know what ministry is like, do you have any desire to go back to the corporate world?"

"Not at all. I love what I'm doing. It's hard work, no doubt about it, but there's an internal satisfaction that means more to me," she replied.

What's the moral of Amanda's story? She reinvented her life, discovered the joy of working on an eternal purpose, and experienced fulfillment by wanting God's will and being honest about the heartfelt wants and desires He put in her heart.

What about you? Your story may look different than Amanda's, but no doubt you also want to discover what God wants for your life. So, let's explore this some more by continuing to answer Reinvent Question #1.

### reinvent question #1: what do you want?

When the Maven was asked, "What shall I do for you?" she voiced her wants to the prophet Elisha. She also learned how to "want what God wants" as she followed the directions she

was given. Rather than questioning the logic, the steps, or the efficiency of God's instructions through the prophet, she chose to want what God wanted and got busy obeying! She may have wondered about the wisdom of borrowing jars from her neighbors or about the craziness of pouring her one little bottle of oil into multiple jars. It didn't make a lot of rational sense. But she wanted to keep her boys and that meant she wanted God's plan more than anything else.

What about you? What do you want? What do you want the Lord to do for you? When He gives you direction, will you trust Him enough to want His will—even if you don't fully understand the rationale behind some of His instructions?

This can be a challenge, especially if *your desire for your will* is stronger than *your desire for His will*. In that case, you'll find yourself being distracted by all kinds of "shiny things." One day you want to be a photographer. The next day, no—you are definitely moving to NYC to be a lifestyle blogger. The following week, you want to minister to orphans in another country. The next month, you're going to travel and snowboard throughout Singapore (except there's no snow and it's 90 percent humidity). The following month you must have more "me time"—and by the end of the year, you want to live in a studio apartment in the mountains and teach hot yoga. And then . . . who knows?

So, how do you dial in to wanting what God wants? Here's a tip: Do what my friend Amanda did by seeking the Lord and spending extra time with Him in prayer and Bible reading. His will is revealed in His Word, so journal any Scriptures and thoughts the Lord quickens to your heart. After thirty days, review your journal notes and watch His will come into focus. Here's what the Lord has promised:

> Delight yourself also in the LORD,
> and **He shall give you the desires of your heart**.
> (Psalm 37:4)

There's a great double-whammy in this passage.

First, when you delight yourself in the Lord (which is to seek, enjoy, and relate to Him), He will put *His desires* in your heart. That means, you'll want what He wants!

Second, as you delight yourself in the Lord, He will guide you with His wisdom to fulfill those desires!

## how do you discern what god wants?

What if you have two or more desires in your heart and they are both good? How do you sort out God's want over your wants? How do you discern what is happening in your heart and your soul? Sometimes, it's a matter of *priority* and other times it's a matter of *timing*.

My friend Mary has been a third-grade teacher in public schools for twenty-nine years. She's won numerous awards and has been a favorite teacher among parents and kids for years. (I can vouch for that; three of our four kids had her as a teacher and she loves all of her students like they are her own.) Halfway through her teaching career, she wondered about other career or ministry options, but ultimately, she wanted what God wanted. She thought about leaving the classroom and earned her master's degree in education administration with hopes of going into an administrative role.

She considered children's ministry options as well, but by prayerfully identifying the desires of her heart over the course of several years, the Lord let her know that teaching in the classroom *was* her mission field. As she put it, "He didn't need me in the jungles of Africa, but rather in the classrooms of America."

She said knowing that makes it fun and rewarding when students and parents come back years later and say they always noticed something different in her relationship with them. "That's when I can give God the glory."

The apostle Paul experienced the dilemma of two desires:

> For to me, to live is Christ, and to die is gain. But if I live on in the flesh, this will mean fruit from my labor; yet what I shall choose I cannot tell. **For I am hard-pressed between the two, having a desire** to depart and be with Christ, which is far better. Nevertheless to remain in the flesh is more needful for you. And being confident of this, I know that I shall remain and continue with you all for your progress and joy of faith. (Philippians 1:21–25)

What's the apostle Paul describing? He's describing what it feels like to have two desires competing within him—and trying to decide which one to choose! One part of him desired to depart (to die and leave this world) and be with Christ. (Sometimes life and ministry are hard, and heaven sure sounds a lot better!)

Interestingly, the word *desire* in this context is from a word that means "forbidden desire." It's also translated many other times in the Bible as "lust." But Paul's other desire was to stay on earth to keep preaching and to reach more people with the gospel of Jesus.

So, how did Paul (and how do we) know which desire is correct? What's the litmus test when we have multiple desires? Or when we want to quit? How do we know if we have a forbidden want? How do we know what God wants? After all, both of Paul's desires were good. It's not a bad thing to want to go be with the Lord and it's not wrong to stay in the world to preach the gospel.

By revelation, Paul came to understand it wasn't the right season (timing) for him to leave this world to go be with Christ. He understood that in the bigger picture of God's purposes, it was more needful (priority) for others that Paul stay on earth and continue preaching the gospel. So, with confidence, He chose what was in the best interest of others, rather than what was best for him!

Years later, when Paul had finished his course and he knew his time on earth was nearing its end, he wrote, "As for me, my life has already been poured out as an offering to God. The time of my death is near. I have fought the good fight, I have finished the race, and I have remained faithful. And now the prize awaits me—the crown of righteousness, which the Lord, the righteous Judge, will give me on the day of his return" (2 Timothy 4:6–8 NLT).

Sometimes, when you have several desires competing for your time and attention, you have to discern between the *timing* and *priority* of those wants.

For example:

- I want to join a softball league, but my wife just had twins. So, this isn't the right time. It's more needful that I stay home and help her.
- I'd love to move to the Swiss Alps, but my best friend just went through a divorce, so it's more needful to stay near my friend for a while.
- I want to sleep in on Sundays, but I was just asked to step into a serving role at my church, so it's more needful that I help further the cause of Christ.

Like everyone, I've also had all kinds of ideas and wants for my life (they usually popped up when I was looking for an escape route from a tough season). Here are a few of mine:

- I want to retire and move to Breckenridge, Colorado, to open up a breakfast restaurant (after I learn how to cook!), but for now, it's more needful for my husband and me to continue pastoring our church family in Kalamazoo.
- I want a total-body makeover, defined arms, and a face-lift, but it's more needful for me to eat right and exercise. (There, I said it.)
- I want to move to Palm Springs to play professional golf, but it's more needful for me to live in reality!

When it comes to answering Reinvent Question #1: What do you want?—there's nothing more fulfilling than being in the center of God's will and wanting what He wants for you! Whether He's called you to be a stay-at-home mom, a corporate executive, a medical professional, a law enforcement officer, a schoolteacher, a news anchor, a college coach, or a country church pastor, remember *it's better to want what God wants*!

## reinvention review

1. How does this chapter and knowing *it's better to want what God wants* free you to reinvent your life?
2. When we delight ourselves in the Lord according to Psalm 37:4, what twofold promise has He given us?
3. How do you discern God's desire when you have two good but competing desires?

## chapter 12

# go after a new bullseye

*It's not who you are that holds you back, it's who you think you're not.*

Denis Waitley

Beauty is more than skin deep. At least that's what Maxwell Maltz, a well-known plastic surgeon in the mid-1900s, observed. He noticed that many of his patients were thrilled with the cosmetic changes they saw after surgery and this was reflected in their happiness. However, others were not pleased after their surgery, and although he showed them before and after photos, they were still not happy about their appearance.

That's when he recognized the image a person had on the inside was more important than his cosmetic work on the outside. If he couldn't change the internal image a person had about themselves, all the surgery in the world couldn't do it either. He also discovered if he could help someone see their beauty on the inside, sometimes they didn't need the cosmetic surgery at all! Indeed, beauty is more than skin deep and the image you see on the inside is actually more important than the image you see on the outside.[1]

I don't know if Dr. Maltz claimed a faith in Jesus Christ, but

his discovery reiterated what the Bible told us all along: "As a man thinks in his heart, so is he" (Proverbs 23:7). He knew his patients *wanted* to be happy, but he realized if they could not see past the image they had of themselves on the inside, they could not experience that happiness. It's such a simple, yet profound biblical truth—as we think in our hearts, so we are! In other words, whatever you believe in your heart about you—is how you *is*! (It's not good English, but true nonetheless.)

Think about it—it doesn't matter if your parents think you're a champ, if your spouse thinks you hung the moon, or if your kids think you're an ATM (*wink*); if *you* don't think these things, you will not experience the benefit. Your friends can tell you you're amazing, those who follow you on social media can love everything you post, complete strangers can say nice things, but if you don't believe it, you won't experience the joy of these realities.

The good news is, you can change what you think!

In order to experience the benefits of seeing yourself and your reinvention the way God does, we need to continue answering Reinvent Question #1.

## reinvent question #1: what do you want?

What do you *want* your life to look like? When it comes to experiencing change, transformation, and reinvention, you'll need a new view of you—a new bullseye to hit! The Maven had to get a fresh vision for improving her life! She had to replace the vision of being a grieving, fearful, widowed single mom of two boys enslaved by her creditors with a new image of herself as a successful, debt-free, confident single mom raising two entrepreneurial boys and loving life! It turns out that a

part of her reinvention included seeing new bullseye targets for her life!

As we get started on this topic, it will be helpful to understand two terms commonly used when it comes to self-improvement. While they are secular expressions, they have biblical roots. Let's look at a basic overview of *self-esteem* and *self-image*.

**Self-esteem.** Self-esteem or self-worth is the value you put on you. How much do you think you are worth? You are God's Masterpiece! Your value is far above rubies (Proverbs 31:10), but sadly, it's reported that 85 percent of the population struggles with low self-esteem.[2]

While people may appear confident and self-assured on the outside, many feel intimidated and inferior on the inside. They don't know their value! Do you?

With all of our flaws, quirks, pain, and shame, God loved us so much He paid the ultimate price by giving His only Son in order to have an eternal relationship with us. We must be more valuable than we sometimes realize.

The value of an item is determined by the price someone is willing to pay for it, right? If I wanted to sell you a cup of coffee and I thought it was worth $20, would you pay $20? Probably not. You would pay what you thought it was worth. Maybe $1? If it was from Starbucks, maybe $5. The price of something is determined by what someone will pay for it.

When God paid the price of His Son to save you from an eternity apart from Him, He declared your value—twice!

First, God the Father believes you are so valuable He was willing to give up His Son to pay for your life.

Second, Jesus Himself believes you are so valuable He was willing to obey His Father and lay down His life to shed His precious blood for you. The price God paid for you declares how valuable you are.

When you recognize your worth, you won't sell yourself short!

**Self-image.** Self-image is different from self-esteem. Self-image is "the image" (or photograph) you *see* of yourself on the inside. In our "selfie" culture, this is not hard to understand. Many people have hundreds of photos of themselves sitting in their phone's camera roll and on their social media feeds. And the truth is, you have an internal camera roll loaded with thousands of "selfies," and these images are neatly organized into internal photo albums, stocked full of self-images.

For example, in your internal camera roll, you have a:

Spiritual Photo Album—with images of how you see yourself spiritually.

Physical Photo Album—you see pictures of yourself physically.

Personality Photo Album—you see selfies of your personality.

You have a Marriage Album, a Parenting Album, a Family Album, a Success Album, a Friend Album, a Calling and Purpose Album, and dozens of other albums all loaded with self-images of how you see yourself.

Why is this important?

## hot targets and heat-seeking missiles

Here's where it gets interesting. The images you have on the inside of you become a "hot-target bullseye" for a "heat-seeking missile"—and as it turns out, YOU are the heat-seeking missile!

You will always hit the target of the image you see on the inside!

In other words, if you see yourself as a happy, smart, and enjoyable person to be around, you'll hit that target. If you see yourself as a grumpy, mean, and miserable person, you'll hit that bullseye. To "hit the target" simply means you'll "automatically"

make choices and act in ways that will enable you to experience, achieve, or realize the thing you see. We are designed to hit the target we see within. We may not even realize the internal course corrections we make every day to hit the target we see.

When people say things like, “Well that’s just how I am,” as an excuse for bad behavior or “I’ve been like this my whole life” as a reason for not changing, what they don’t know is that this is not how they *are*; this is their bullseye—this is the target they *see* themselves hitting.

If you *see* yourself as a strong Christian, a loving spouse, an encouraging parent, and a caring person, you’ll hit that target. On the other hand, if you have an internal image of yourself as a double-minded believer, an angry person, a nit-picking parent, or a fault-finding boss, you’ll hit that target, too—automatically!

Maltz described this heat-seeking missile concept as an automatic success mechanism within us: “Every living thing has a built-in guidance system or goal striving device, put there by its Creator to help it achieve its goal.”[3]

Athletes have known about the importance of the internal images they see for years and often golfers and basketball players will “play” the golf course or “shoot” the winning shot over and over in their mind before they ever set foot on the golf course or basketball court. They create “muscle memory” by imagining their performance. The same has been seen when helping stroke patients regain use of limbs.

In his book *The God-Shaped Brain*, Timothy Jennings, MD, explains how our brains are wired and the power of what people see, imagine, or visualize within: “Brain science has given us some insights into the amazing pathways through which our thoughts actually change our brain.” He goes on to say,

In 2007 brain research revealed that the same brain circuits that activate to painful stimuli also activate when people imagine painful stimuli. In 2000, Kark Herholz and Wolf-Dieter Heiss discovered that stroke patients who merely imagined moving an affected limb actually activated the corresponding neural circuits in their brains. This is the concept of visualization in artistic and athletic performance: brain studies have shown that when musicians imagine playing a piece of music, the same motor pathways activate as if they were actually playing their instrument, even though no muscles are being used. **The thoughts we think actually reshape our brains.**[4]

## see it and say it

It's not just what we *see*; it's what we *say*, too. On her blog, Dr. Caroline Leaf describes it this way:

> Today, there is an increasing body of evidence that the brain changes according to experience. The anatomy and physiology of the human brain is much more malleable and plastic than we once thought—the brain changes according to how we use it! Yes, life can certainly be challenging, but our minds are actually more than prepared to stand up to these challenges and overcome them—all we have to do is think! Our ability to think is truly phenomenal. Our brains can change as we think (neuroplasticity) and grow new brain cells (neurogenesis). Using the incredible power in our minds, we can persist and grow in response to life's challenges. **We can take our thoughts captive and change the way we think, speak and act!**[5]

Did you catch that? We can change the way we think, speak, and act! These principles are described in the Bible—it's what takes place in our mind when *thoughts* become *imaginations* and *imaginations* become *strongholds* and *strongholds* become the *target* we hit (2 Corinthians 10:3–5). The crazy part is it doesn't matter if the thoughts, imaginations, or strongholds are good or bad—we are neurologically wired to hit them. (Of course, it does matter in real life!)

If you have an internal image of yourself as a rejected failure, you'll hit that target. If you have an internal photo of yourself as a favored success, you'll hit that target, too.

That's why the question, "What do you want?" is so vital. You control the image you see and the words you say and the bullseye you hit.

With this in mind, what images are in your photo albums? More importantly, if those selfies are the target that you, as the "heat-seeking missile," don't want to hit, how do you replace and exchange those images? We can replace every ungodly, negative, and self-defeating internal image we have with a victorious, positive, and godly one simply by believing, seeing, and saying what God says about us. Thankfully, He's given us thousands of "stock images" in His Word—we need to get them uploaded to our internal hard drive!

Let me tell you a few embarrassing stories of how this principle works. Through a series of unconnected events, certain images made their way to my inner photo albums and the self-defeating results motivated me to replace them. No doubt, you have a few images like this as well. I want to share how the Lord helped me replace those photos and reinvent my life, because if these principles worked for me, they will work in your life, too.

### prom

It was my senior year in high school and I really *wanted* to go to prom, but I wasn't dating anyone, and no one had asked me to go. A selfie—a hot-target bullseye—was being developed within my internal Love Life Photo Album. It looked like this: *No one wants you.*

As prom drew closer, a guy named Kurt randomly asked me to play tennis. He was two years older than me and had already graduated from high school. I knew him casually, as he was the son of a friend of my dad's. When we were playing tennis, he asked me if I was going to my school prom. I told him no one had asked me. He said, "Would you like to go with me?" I couldn't believe it! Really? I said, "Yes!" I didn't know Kurt very well, but he was a gentleman and I was thrilled to go to prom. I borrowed a long, smoky-gray dress from a friend and woven brown leather huarache sandals from my sister (my fashion re-invention came later). Kurt wore a lemon-yellow tux and off we went! We had a great time.

Ten years later, one of my sisters casually commented, "Wasn't that nice of Dad to ask Kurt to take you to the prom?"

I was like, "Wait, what? Dad *asked* Kurt to take me???" I couldn't believe it! But that's not the end of the story.

"Yes," my sister said, "didn't you know? Dad paid Kurt one hundred dollars!"

"Whaaat? He *paid* him a hundred bucks???" Now I *was* mortified! Are you kidding me?

I was shocked and embarrassed, and it just sharpened the *no one wants you* image within me. (Strangely, in the very same moment, I thought it was nice of my dad to step in to help me go to prom. For all I know, my dad probably paid for the prom tickets, corsage, and dinner, too!)

**"they all want me bad"**

Fast-forward a few years. My youngest sister, Michelle, got engaged! She was the first of my three sisters to get married. I am the oldest of four girls, so you know where this story is going. The next sister to get engaged was Rhonda, the second oldest. Then it was my third sister, Kelly. When you're the oldest sister and all three of your younger sisters are engaged and married and you are not even dating anyone, that's not cool! It's humiliating and slightly devastating. It didn't help that at every wedding, sometime during the reception, someone made a beeline to ask me the fateful question: "And when are you going to get married?" (*#cringe*) "I have no earthly idea! For the love of God, why are you asking me this ridiculous question?" is what I wanted to say. All the while, I could feel the *no one wants you* selfie multiplying.

Oh, the plot thickens.

Within a two-year window of my sisters all being married, my two best friends were also engaged and married. I was in all five weddings and had a nice bridesmaid dress collection going. I was genuinely happy for all of them—but by the fifth wedding, the *no one wants you* image was confirmed, enlarged, laminated, and animated. I was locked on and hitting the target. (Don't get me wrong, I had several dates along the way. One guy I dated actually interviewed me to see if I would make for a good pastor's wife/secretary. Yes, seriously. *#LouisvilleSluggertobothheadlightscomestomind*)

Finding true love seemed further and further away.

Until . . . the Lord helped me to replace the photos!

I happened to read this Scripture: "Search from the book of the Lord, and read: Not one of these shall fail; **Not one shall lack her mate**. For My mouth has commanded it, and **His Spirit has**

**gathered them**" (Isaiah 34:16). Although this passage is talking about animals and their mates, I grabbed on to it and claimed it for myself, because you know what they say? *Desperate times call for desperate measures!*

I *wanted* to meet my mate and it was in my best interest to *see it* and *say it*! This passage sealed the deal for me:

> Death and life are in the power of the tongue,
> and those who love it will eat its fruit.
> **He who finds a wife finds a good thing,**
> and obtains favor from the LORD. (Proverbs 18:21–22)

When I thought about these passages, a new selfie came to my mind—I *saw* my husband searching for me and I *saw* the Spirit gathering me to my husband. This was my new internal bullseye.

How could I summarize it into a faith-filled phrase I could *say*? I came up with a sentence, but now should I say it? Is it too ridiculous? I thought it over. One day, I finally said it. I blurted it out to my roommate, Mary Jo: "They all want me... bad!" I laughed and said it again! "They all want me bad!" Mary Jo joined me, and we laughed and laughed. This was the bullseye I needed my husband to hit!

When I said, "They all want me bad" the first couple of times, I *wanted* to believe it, but I just said it by faith, hoping one day someone would want me. It was a start.

This is where reinvention gets real. The old images were taunting me: *No one wants you! Who are you trying to kid?* The new photo I'd just installed piped up: *They all want you bad! Remember?* What was I going to do? Believe the old images that had only discouraged me and been a bullseye I was hitting, or would I have enough faith to believe God could do something new, something different in my life?

I believed. I continued installing this new selfie bullseye by seeing and saying what I *wanted* that target to be. In the morning as I was doing my hair, I'd tell Mary Jo, "They all want me...bad!" When I was driving to work, I said it out loud: "They all want me bad." When the old *no one wants you* image tried to pipe up, I said it again louder: "They all want me bad!"

And do you know, that hot target got hotter and I found myself starting to believe it! (Keep in mind, when I said, "They all want me bad," I didn't literally believe every guy would want to date me, but I did believe the one right guy would!)

Several months after saying, "They all want me bad," one day when I said it, I actually believed it! I believed my husband was going to find me and the Lord was ordering my steps to him—and he was going to want me bad!

Then, it happened!

I hit the new target...or the new target hit me! Through a series of events, I met Jeff Jones and we started dating. He was more than I had asked for: he was tall, good-looking, hilarious, and successful; he loved the Lord; he treated me like a queen; and he drove a sweet, "rich man's" car—a cream-colored Buick Riviera, with tan leather!

I remembered Jeff from high school; he was two years older than me and one of those cool upperclassmen. We'd been out of high school for over ten years and had not really known each other, but when we met, it didn't take long (forty days to be exact!) until we were engaged and then married eight months after that. *#bullseye*

A few weeks before we were married, on a date one night he said, "I want you bad!" I could not believe my ears! Did he literally just say those words? He did! He didn't even know about my crazy story! I smiled toward heaven and winked. "Thank You, Lord—it worked!" For over thirty years now, we've

enjoyed a marriage made in heaven, and it's been the best twenty-eight years of our lives. (Married people, you understand that math.)

I tell you all of these embarrassing stories to encourage you. No matter what images you've had in your internal photo albums and no matter what bullseye targets you've been hitting—I know this principle of replacing old images with new targets based on God's Word will work for you! What bullseye targets do you want to hit? What will you begin to see and say?

When it comes to Reinvent Question #1: What do you want?—if you'll believe it, see it, and say it, you'll be able to *go after a new bullseye* and reinvent your life!

## reinvention review

1. Can you see how *going after a new bullseye* will revolutionize your reinvention game plan? How?
2. If it's true that as a man thinks in his heart, so is he—what new targets do you want to hit and what new photos do you need to install in the photo albums of your life?
3. If it's true that the power of life and death is in our tongue, what phrase could you believe, see, and say to hit the bullseye targets you desire?

# chapter 13

# go small and stay home

*Great things are done by a series of small things brought together.*

Vincent van Gogh

I loved my small van—okay, *minivan*! I was one of those few people, with kids in middle and high school, who still had a minivan and loved it! Until one day. I was on a road trip when a Lexus SUV passed me, and I thought, *Now, that's a nice car—I'd love a car like that!*

I wasn't actually looking for a car, but it turns out, a car was looking for me! As I admired the passing Lexus casually expressing my desire, I heard a *still, small voice* that said, "Go get one." I laughed and said to myself, "Right, I'll just go do that!" while inwardly thinking, *We don't have the money for me to "just go get" a Lexus*. But just as quickly, I felt the Holy Spirit's challenge: "Since when are you trusting in what you have? What if I want to reward you?" This was probably just me trying to justify a Lexus, right? I wondered. But the more I thought about a Lexus and pondered the idea God may have actually spoken to my heart, the more excited I got. So, what did I do?

I did what I'd normally do when I thought the Lord was

speaking to my heart. I "pretended" I heard from God and began to take *small steps* to see what He opened up—after all, if I didn't take any steps, nothing was going to happen for sure!

My first step? I went to visit a local Lexus dealer to test-drive an SUV. I'd never been in a Lexus and I wanted to see how it felt. Well (surprise, surprise!), I loved it, but it was out of my price range. I went home and prayerfully pondered what to do and how the Lord wanted me to "just go get one."

I decided to search for a Lexus SUV on eBay. (Mind you, up until this point I'd never bought anything over $50 on eBay!) Within a few weeks, I found a newer hybrid Lexus SUV with 8,000 miles on eBay, at a substantially lower price than at the local dealer. Well, you know what happened, right? I got the thumbs-up from my husband, sold my minivan, and with a healthy down payment, we secured a loan from our bank to buy the Lexus on eBay. Needless to say, I loved that Lexus and was reminded of God's goodness every time I drove it!

Several years later, just after it was paid off, the Lord spoke to my heart again with His *still, small voice*: "I'd like you to give your Lexus to a pastor's wife." Because I knew the Lexus had been a reward to me from the Lord, I was actually excited about the prospect of giving this car to reward another pastor's wife. I talked to my husband about it and again got the thumbs-up from him. So I asked the Lord, "Who? What pastor's wife?" As I pondered this question, a certain pastor's wife came to my mind and heart. I contacted her husband to see what he thought about the idea. He told me his wife had been going through a very difficult time and this would be a huge blessing to remind her God had not forgotten her. We decided on a date to "accidentally" meet up at a local coffee shop to surprise her with the car. What a fun experience that was! The surprise worked out

perfectly and she was so happy. But the truth is, I was even more blessed, because just like Jesus said, it's truly "more blessed to give than to receive!"

As I pondered what I was going to do for my next car, guess what the Lord said? He said, "Go get what you *want*!" So I did. A four-door, white Jeep Wrangler Sahara with a removable top and doors!

This whole story may not sound ultra-dramatic—after all, this isn't a story about giving away a Lexus so a Lamborghini or a Maserati would drop from the heavens. But that's the whole point—it's an everyday story about the thrill of a faith adventure, of listening for the Lord's *still, small voice* and taking *small steps* to partner with the Lord.

What has the Lord been saying to you through His still, small voice? What small steps do you need to take? Let's continue answering Reinvent Question #1.

## reinvent question #1: what do you want?

What do you want the Lord to do for you? Maybe this is a good time to "go small and stay home." Wait! Don't we mean "go big or go home"? After all, we live in a "think big" and "all things are possible with God" world, right?

Thinking big is good, but sometimes we can be so focused on the big stuff, the greatest hit, the bestseller, the blockbuster, and the championship that we miss and dismiss the power of the small. What if you *wanted* small things? Let me stir you up with a variety of stories and see what types of small ideas come to your heart.

Don't forget the Maven had only a *small* jar of anointing oil—but it was through that small jar that God did big things!

Sometimes we stress ourselves out trying to go big, when maybe what we really *want* to do is go small!

Seth Godin captured this idea in his book *Small Is the New Big*. He introduces hundreds of novel aha thoughts about small things! He tells us Jeff Bezos named his company Amazon because it starts with an *A* and would be first in the alphabetical list or phone book! That's a small (but big) thing! He reminded us that small companies can do big things—case in point: eBay has 14,000 employees (big) and Craigslist only has fifty (small).[1]

You can go small and stay home in order to see BIG results!

## the long tail

There's a theory in marketing called the "long tail." It's not about having the "bestseller" for a few months; it's about having the "consistent seller" for many years.

Think about it this way.

Back in the early days of television, most people had access to three channels—if you had rabbit ears (or a hanger and aluminum foil you stuck in the antennae port), you might be able to pull in a few more channels. The only way to survive on those few TV shows back then was to be a big star, have a huge budget, and develop an award-winning program. A few people make a splash for a short time. This is the short tail.

Today, with thousands of channels for delivering content, you don't have to be a big star or heavily connected to succeed in television. These days, anyone with a decent digital camera, a video editing app, and a multi-channel marketing strategy can launch a television, video, or on-demand program to reach a small segment of the market. A lot of people can make a consistent impact for a long time. This is known as the long tail.

The Internet and social media have leveled the playing field and given us the ability to reach multiple markets with products and services! You don't have to be a well-known movie star, author, manufacturer, or name brand—you can be an unknown individual who is crazy enough to believe in your story or product. Just tap into the long tail of these opportunities and reinvent your life!

Amanda Hocking has never been a *New York Times* best-selling author who sells millions of books, but when she was twenty-six years old and unable to get a big publisher to look at her material, she self-published her fiction work in an e-book format on Kindle. You may or may not be a fan of her genre, but she sold these e-books for anywhere between ninety-nine cents and three dollars, and they caught on! She kept writing and maximizing the opportunity on the Internet. At one time, she had nine e-books selling 450,000 copies a month! Today, she's a millionaire and keeps selling! That's the long tail![2]

Do you want to impact the world around you? Do you have a book, a program, a movie, a message, an expertise, a product, a service, a talent, or a business to share with the world? Why not "go small and stay home"?

Let me share a personal example. In 1988, I wrote *Getting a Grip on the Basics*, a Bible study workbook to strengthen believers in the basics of their faith. After I finished writing the book, I asked the Lord to use the book as He saw fit, and here's how our conversation went:

> "Lord, I ask You to use this book and get it into the hands of anyone in America who needs to be established in the basics of their faith. Lord, use it to help Your church and to build up Your body. In Jesus's name. Amen."

I heard the Lord speak to my heart: "Why stop with America?"

"Okay, Lord, I ask You to use this book and get it into the hands of anyone who speaks English who needs to be established in the basics of their faith. Lord use it to help Your church and to build up Your body. In Jesus's name. Amen."

Again, I heard the Lord speak to my heart, "Why stop with English?"

"Okay, Father, I ask You to use this book and get it into the hands of anyone, anywhere on planet earth and in any language You see fit, to strengthen them in the basics of their faith. Lord, use it to help Your church and to build up Your body. In Jesus's name. Amen."

Finally, I heard the Lord speak, "Why stop with earth?" (JK. He didn't say that part.)

Now, over thirty years later, He has seen fit to get this book into nations around the world by prompting people to translate it into twenty languages and counting. Here's the long tail part of the story. This book has never been a *New York Times* bestseller, and most people wouldn't even know this book exists, but with more than 250,000 English copies circulating, it's been in the long tail for decades. The best part of the long tail is that this book is still going to nations, villages, and homes I'll never visit this side of heaven, but the Lord is using the book to strengthen people in the basics of their faith.

What does this mean for you? It means you can see great success in the long tail of whatever area of your life you *want* to reinvent, by *going small and staying home*!

## 1,000 true fans

In 2008, Kevin Kelly wrote a blog that went viral. He described the power of 1,000 true fans as an income model. Do you want to reinvent your business or influence? Rather than trying to reach millions of people, the idea is to go small by acquiring, serving, and nurturing 1,000 true fans who love you or your product, content, or service. Do the math and you'll see that if you inspire 1,000 true fans to purchase $100 worth of goods each year, you could earn an income of $100,000 annually. Here it is in Kelly's own words:

> To be a successful creator you don't need millions. You don't need millions of dollars or millions of customers, millions of clients or millions of fans. To make a living as a craftsperson, photographer, musician, designer, author, animator, app maker, entrepreneur, or inventor you need only thousands of true fans. A true fan is defined as a fan that will buy anything you produce. These diehard fans will drive 200 miles to see you sing; they will buy the hardback and paperback and audible versions of your book; they will purchase your next figurine sight unseen; they will pay for the "best-of" DVD version of your free YouTube channel; they will come to your chef's table once a month. If you have roughly a thousand true fans like this (also known as super fans), you can make a living—if you are content to make a living but not a fortune. Here's how the math works. You need to meet two criteria. First, you have to create enough each year that you can earn, on average, $100 profit from each true fan. That is easier to do in some arts and businesses than others, but it is a good creative challenge in every area because it is always easier

and better to give your existing customers more, than it is to find new fans.[3]

To attract 1,000 true fans requires you to have a product, cause, service, or business that adds value to people's lives. With the help of your smartphone and a few creative business, marketing, and financial apps, you can literally reach anyone, anywhere in the world. By employing Kevin Kelly's 1,000 True Fans model along with God's wisdom and consistent, strategic effort, you can go small and stay home.

Seth Godin describes it this way: "If you can figure out how to embrace the true fans, they'll go ahead and spread an idea—not because you want them to, but because they want to. Your ability to reach a tiny group of committed fans is essential. But the work spreads because of the fans, not because you figured out how to spend money to interrupt more and more strangers." This approach to going small isn't about more dollars being thrown at mass market advertising—it's about building value-oriented relationships one person at a time.[4]

## little things are big things

Remember one of the heroes I told you about earlier? I mentioned a successful businessman we admired and who recently graduated to heaven, but over the course of his life, he anonymously made it possible for 5,000 kids to attend a Christian summer camp. The surprising secret to his success, wealth, and influence? He didn't try to "go big" by swinging for the fences or hitting home runs in massive business deals; instead he chose to "go small" by consistently hitting one single after another, after

another, after another. In doing so, he achieved *heroic* success and was able to share it with others.

What about Sandra Bullock's sister? Of course, we all know the famous A-list actress and director Sandra Bullock, but what about Gesine, her sister? Gesine went to law school and while she was supposed to be studying for the bar exam, she was baking. After she passed the bar, she realized law was not her passion. She really *wanted* to bake. So, she packed up her stuff and moved to Vermont and opened up a school to teach people how to bake. The Food Network heard about her and launched her into TV with a program called *Baked in Vermont*. She's not making blockbuster movies like her sister, but she's been very successful following her passion and focusing on her niche. She went small and stayed home![5]

What if you decided to "go small and stay home" literally? What could you do from the comfort of your sofa, in your PJs, with your laptop? Our daughter Meghan (@mrshock) is doing just that. As a stay-at-home mom, with savvy computer skills, she's selling the items in her closet online through Poshmark. After she got started, it didn't take long until she became one of their featured sellers, with upward of 300,000 followers. It's a nice little side hustle, where she gets to leverage the Internet and the beauty of going small and staying home!

I love this verse of Scripture: "Do not despise these **small beginnings**, for the Lord rejoices to see the work begin" (Zechariah 4:10 NLT). The Lord rejoices to see the work begin!

When it comes to Reinvent Question #1: What do you want?—remember, small is the new big. You can *go small and stay home*!

But what if you want to go big? Maybe you have political aspirations? Always wanted to be a brain surgeon? A member of SEAL Team Six? Start a camp for special needs kids? Write a

Broadway musical? Want to change the culture? All of the big things start small! What if you have big dreams in your heart? No worries. Let's shift gears and talk about going big!

## reinvention review

1. How does the idea of *going small and staying home* help you to rethink and reconsider your options for reinventing?
2. What thoughts or ideas has the Lord been speaking to you through His still, small voice?
3. Do you have a product, book, teaching, service, or idea that could benefit from the long tail concept? Describe it.

chapter 14

# go big and work on your magnum opus

*If people aren't calling you crazy, you aren't thinking big enough.*

Richard Branson

While visiting Rome and the Vatican City a few years ago, we couldn't help but stand in awe at the works of Michelangelo. We were fortunate to see both the *Pietà* as well as the ceiling and altar wall of the Sistine Chapel. It's hard to know which of his multiple works are actually his magnum opus.

By definition, a *magnum opus* is "the great work; the greatest achievement of an artist or writer."[1]

Many people regard the *Pietà*—the marble sculpture of Mary, the mother of Jesus, holding His body after the crucifixion and before He was placed in the tomb—as his greatest work, his magnum opus. (It is the only work he signed.) Concerning his incredible gift to sculpt, Michelangelo said, "The sculpture is already complete within the marble block, before I start my work. It is already there, I just have to chisel away the superfluous material."[2]

And while the *Pietà* could very well be Michelangelo's magnum

opus, the Sistine Chapel is a strong contender. It is surreal. Both the ceiling, and its depiction of nine different points of the Book of Genesis, and the altar wall (which he painted twenty-five years later) with the Last Great Judgment and the Second Coming of Christ are truly breathtaking.

The marvel of the Sistine Chapel is not only the incredible talent and detail required, but also the positions from which Michelangelo had to paint it! He painted the ceiling while on scaffolding, some say lying on his back. It took him four years and he nearly went blind.[3]

It's no surprise that some consider the Sistine Chapel to be the most visited room in the world, with upward of five million people a year stopping by to be awestruck. That's what a magnum opus does: It's a great work that strikes people with awe.

What if God wants to do big things in and through you, too? It's possible! Let's wrap up answering Reinvent Question #1 by talking about it.

## reinvent question #1: what do you want?

Why not think big and work on *your* magnum opus? (Sounds a bit pretentious, doesn't it? It's not.) By definition, your magnum opus is what *you* regard as your most important work. It's not what others think or how they esteem you or your work; it's what you view as your greatest achievement. Your magnum opus is your legacy. The reason you were born. It's what you are leaving behind.

The Maven got a taste of a big life when God touched and multiplied her oil and then filled the many empty jars! He set her and her boys up for a big future in oil! This must have been her magnum opus, as it's the only record we have of her and what she left behind!

What do you want to leave behind as your magnum opus? Do you have a creative desire within you? A desire to paint, sculpt, write, sing, design, serve, preach, or build something that will impact people for years to come? Why not work on *your* magnum opus? Somebody has to design buildings. Write music. Paint masterpieces. Why not you?

In Barcelona, Spain, the enormous Sagrada Familia cathedral is breathtaking and dominates the skyline. Amazingly, it has been under construction for over 136 years! (Yes, you read that right!) It's not projected to be completed until 2026. Each year, over three million people visit this church building designed by architect Antoni Gaudí, the most famous architect in all of Barcelona. Mr. Gaudi passed away in 1926, but no doubt the Sagrada Familia is his magnum opus! Not only is the architecture beautiful, but also inside the Sagrada Familia all of the architecture does one thing—it points to Jesus.

> The original design calls for eighteen spires to symbolize the Twelve Apostles, Virgin Mary, Four Evangelists, and Jesus Christ. The spires increase in height to visually represent the hierarchy of these religious figures. When it's completely constructed—the tallest spire representing Jesus Christ will give the church its full height of 560 feet. This will put it just slightly shorter than Montjuïc hill, Barcelona's highest point. It was an intentional decision by the architect, who felt that nothing made by man should surpass what was made by God.[4]

Ludwig van Beethoven is considered one of the greatest composers of all time. Over the course of forty-five years, he composed 722 works, but his Symphony no. 9 in D Minor (or

Beethoven's Ninth) is regarded by most as his magnum opus—his greatest work.[5]

We can't forget Leonardo da Vinci's *Mona Lisa*, considered his magnum opus and arguably the most famous painting in the world. The painting itself is only 30 x 20 7/8 inches and yet it has captured the hearts of millions. Featured in its own secure, climate-controlled space in the Louvre in Paris, it draws six million people each year and they spend an average of only fifteen seconds looking at her.[6]

All of these works *are* incredible! But if the magnum opuses of these iconic, historic figures have you feeling a little intimidated, let's scale it down.

## spiders and billionaires

How would you like to be inspired by a spider? Do you remember the story of *Charlotte's Web*?

> "Are you awake, Charlotte?" he said softly.
>
> "Yes," came the answer.
>
> "What is that nifty little thing? Did you make it?"
>
> "I did indeed," replied Charlotte in a weak voice.
>
> "Is it a plaything?"
>
> "Plaything? I should say not. It is my egg sack, my magnum opus."
>
> "I don't know what a magnum opus is," said Wilbur.
>
> "That's Latin," explained Charlotte. "It means great work. This egg sack is my great work, the finest thing I've ever made."
>
> "What's inside of it?" asked Wilbur. "Eggs?"
>
> "Five hundred and fourteen of them," said Charlotte.[7]

Charlotte understood her magnum opus. Five hundred and fourteen little baby spiders! (Sounds more like a magnum nightmare!)

Maybe you're not a classical composer, a sculptor, an architect... or a spider, but you do have the Creator of the ends of the earth living within you!

You may not have the desire or talent to create big things, but you do have a big heart to help someone else do it—serving another can be your magnum opus. In fact, Jesus said to be great (big) in God's kingdom, you have to be the servant of all. Maybe it's the high calling of raising your kids, or your grandkids. Or like Anna of the Bible, you've spent a lifetime praying for God's kingdom to come on earth as it is in heaven. This is brilliant! Talk about legacy. The *family* and the *church* are two of the most important "institutions" God ever established.

In all of the above, God sees your potential and by the power of the Holy Spirit He can help you "remove the excess stone" to free the magnum opus that already exists within you!

To stir you up in your magnum opus... let me give you two words: *think billions*!

Larry Page from Google said, "If you're changing the world, you're working on important things. You're excited to get up in the morning."[8] That's true! Are you excited about getting up in the morning? If not, just think a little bigger and start changing the world. (Right. That's all.)

For a moment, think about what it would be like to solve problems for one billion people! That's what Google, Amazon, Bill and Melinda Gates, Elon Musk, and other billionaires ARE thinking about!

Jesus told a parable about the people of this world who are sometimes more shrewd than His followers (Luke 16:8).

As believers, we need to be as shrewd—sharp, perceptive,

intelligent, clever, aware, and observant—as the world. So, where are these shrewd Christian billionaires? Inventors? Innovators? Culture-shapers? World-changers? Where are the modern-day Abrahams, Davids, Esthers, and Pauls? They could be you!

Thankfully, God has raised up many Christian influencers around the globe. I love reading stories of celebrity actors, singers, news anchors, politicians, social media influencers, models, entrepreneurs, and athletes who are strong in their Christian faith and following God's wisdom to boldly influence those in their sphere. It takes God's reinventive power and faith to go big. I believe He wants to raise up many, many more people with this kind of influence in these days—why not you?

I was inspired (and slightly exhausted!) reading Amazon's annual report; their accomplishments and goals for world domination are massive and real! Several years ago, I read Bill and Melinda Gates's Annual Letter and again was further challenged. They don't have a goal to help a few needy and less fortunate people; they have a goal to eradicate poverty and change entire nations! And it's not a pie-in-the-sky vision; they are putting human and financial resources behind it.[9]

If, as Jesus said, all things are possible to those who believe, what can you believe? What do you believe? Do you want to change the world for one billion people? You could!

## big things start small

Every big faith adventure starts small.

We had a big vision, but we started small. When my husband and I first started out in pastoring, we were thankful when literally "tens of people" showed up! While Jeff is a phenomenal pastor and teacher now, when we first started, he freely admits

he was so boring he didn't want to listen to himself! I tried to be encouraging, but I was so busy growing our kids' ministry from one to two (only because our daughter Meghan brought her friend Rachel!) I had to encourage myself! We spent one year in our ministry journey working our tails off and the church only grew by five people! (Five precious souls, but still.)

Eventually our small church got bigger and every season of growth required Spirit-led reinvention. Whether it was personal reinvention He was working in our own lives or a reinvention in the methods of ministry we employed, when we followed His lead, we eventually saw a season of growth.

Over the past several decades, we've been blessed by the incredibly gifted and servant-hearted staff and volunteers who have come alongside to help us fulfill His vision. Some of those people have been "lifers" with us for the whole journey, while others have been with us for a God-designed season. When I think about those who've labored with us over the years, and are now in heaven, enjoying their reward, I can't help but believe the fruit that accumulates through the church is continually being credited to their magnum opus account in heaven!

It's been almost thirty years and our church has grown from the original five adults and four kids in a small, rented building to reaching thousands of people weekly on our beautiful property. In addition, the Lord has opened many doors for us to take the gospel beyond Kalamazoo—through books, podcasts, and a global television program. We thought we had a big vision when we started, but I never dreamed our Bible study books would be available in Chinese, Korean, Russian, Farsi, and sixteen other languages. However, God did! I never imagined teaching the Bible on television in Iran, Afghanistan, or Tajikistan—let alone in the United States, the UK, Africa, or Australia—but God did.

The truth is, our success, while big to us, is small by some standards. It's not uncommon in various places around the world for churches to be 30,000 to 90,0000 people strong and meeting in multiple sites each week.

What kind of a vision has the Lord given you? Whether you're starting small by reaching "tens of people" or you're reaching thousands in a small town like Kalamazoo or tens of thousands in a big city like Seoul, Singapore, or Sydney—it's all significant to God.

God has a big vision for *you* to fulfill and you can do it (Ephesians 3:20). You've got the goods! There is a world-changing leader within you and the Lord is working His magnum opus in your life by chiseling away the superfluous material. I want to challenge you: Go big and work on your magnum opus! Why not pray, believe, and get busy reaching ~~one million~~ one billion people?

## the biggest magnum opus

As we wrap up this chapter, let's remind ourselves that the greatest work of our lives—the biggest magnum opus of all—is simply this: to know God.

Jesus said so:

> And this is eternal life, that they may know You, the only true God, and Jesus Christ whom You have sent. (John 17:3)

Dr. Caroline Leaf (have I mentioned I like her?) put it simply: "We are wired for love. We are actually designed to be addicted to God."[10]

God made us that way. The psalmist knew something about *wanting* God: "Whom have I in heaven but you? You're all I want! No one on earth means as much to me as you" (Psalm 73:25 TPT).

Even if the Lord fulfilled all your big dreams and desires—gave you a better job, more influence, cooler friends, a new house, a big yacht, a youthful body, and a trip to Bora Bora—if you've not found your true satisfaction in Him, there would still be a gaping hole in your heart and you'd ask, "Is this all there is?" That's because there really is a God-shaped hole in all of us.

Blaise Pascal, the famous French mathematician, physicist, and inventor, put it best: "There is a God-shaped vacuum in the heart of every man which cannot be filled by any created thing but only by God the Creator, made known through Jesus Christ."[11]

The idea that Jesus could be what we *want* is often a theoretical nicety, but not reality for many followers of Jesus. Jesus doesn't want any of His followers to "fake it"—He wants you and I to experience the real and true fulfillment that comes from knowing Him.

> For **he satisfies** the longing soul,
> and the hungry soul he fills with good things. (Psalm 107:9 ESV)

Sometimes, we need a *magnum refresher* in our relationship with the Lord. If you've been pursuing things that satisfy your soul and body but leave your spirit dry, why not have a conversation with the Lord to tell Him what you really, really *want* when it comes to your relationship with Him?

We've taken several chapters to answer Reinvent Question #1:

What do you want?—I hope your wheels are spinning and God is enlarging your heart's desires and vision to *go big and work on your magnum opus*!

Now, let's jump into Reinvent Question #2.

## reinvention review

1. In what ways does the potential to *go big and work on your magnum opus* inspire you?
2. What are the biggest dreams and desires you've ever had? What type of legacy would you like to leave? Why not write it down in a journal or notebook and begin praying for God's wisdom and leading to see it come to pass?
3. What would you do with $1 million? $1 billion?

section 6

# reinvent question #2: *what do you have?*

# chapter 15

# possessions and quirks

*Start where you are. Use what you have. Do what you can.*

Arthur Ashe, U.S. Open and Wimbledon Champion

The whole world enjoyed a collective mic-drop moment when Susan Boyle hit the stage on *Britain's Got Talent* over ten years ago. She was quirky and nervous (and who wouldn't be in that circumstance!). Before she sang a note, you could see the judges raise an eyebrow, not expecting much from this unique lady. But when Susan Boyle opened her mouth to sing "I Dreamed a Dream," the woman *possessed* an anointed voice! When Simon Cowell's jaw dropped in utter happy disbelief, we all became fans! This incredible moment was the reinvention launch of her career. This woman who possessed the voice of an angel later revealed her struggle with Asperger syndrome.[1]

In talking about her diagnosis of Asperger's, she said, "It's nothing to be ashamed of. Everybody has something. I mean, a flaw, if you like. But you shouldn't be ashamed of it. It's something that you bring out in the open in the hope that you help other people. I like to feel I'm the voice for people

who have been the underdog, and I wanted to try and prove myself."[2]

What's true of Susan Boyle is true of you, too—we all have unique possessions and we all have unique quirks. What if God wants to use (and even anoint!) your uniqueness to reinvent your life and help you reach your God-given potential?

Let's revisit the Maven's story to talk about Reinvent Question #2: What do you have? Over the next several chapters, let's take inventory of our assets and blessings in these areas:

Possessions and Quirks
Passions and Purpose
Friends and Cronies
Family and Kinfolk

## reinvent question #2: what do you have?

> A certain woman of the wives of the sons of the prophets cried out to Elisha, saying, "Your servant my husband is dead, and you know that your servant feared the LORD. And the creditor is coming to take my two sons to be his slaves."
>
> So Elisha said to her, "What shall I do for you? Tell me, **what do you have in the house?**" And she said, "Your maidservant has nothing in the house but a jar of oil." (2 Kings 4:1–2)

"What do you have?" This is the second question we must ask as we reinvent our lives.

The instinctive answer of the Maven was very much like our answers at times: "I don't have *anything*... well, except this jar

of oil!" We often feel what we have is so insignificant compared to the needs we have in our lives: "Move along. Nothing to see here. I've got nothing. Nothing of value here."

But the truth is, she did have some things. She probably had a table and chairs and woven placemats and a bed and maybe a few dresses and a closet full of sandals. Maybe she had cookware, dishes, and a Hebrew-press coffee maker? (You never know?!) It wasn't like she didn't have *anything*. But none of those things had value when it came to the reinvention of her life.

When she thought about what she had of value—the jar of oil came to her mind. Why? Most scholars believe the Maven's little pot of oil was used for anointing, not cooking. She *had* a jar of anointing oil and this is the very thing God touched, multiplied, and monetized! It was that small, seemingly insignificant jar of oil that was touched with God's influence and, ultimately, reinvented her life. By recognizing the anointing (oil) she had, she was able to start fresh and love life. *#truthbomb* Did you catch that?

## your jar of anointing oil

The good news is, although at first glance you may also feel you don't *have* anything God could use to reinvent your life, you actually *have* more than you realize. You, too, have a *jar of anointing oil*.

You can look at your jar of anointing oil in several ways. Your jar of oil can be likened to the anointing and ability God has given you (like your anointing to sing, preach, build, or create), and it can be compared to the anointed touch God puts on the things you have (like His anointing on your expertise, voice, or family).

Yes, like the Maven, you, too, have an anointed *something*. It's probably not a jar of oil, but you have other anointings—and God wants to touch, multiply, and monetize what you *have*—to reinvent your life, in the most fruitful and fulfilling way.

Let's delve into this a bit. We won't get into the deep, theological weeds on the "anointing"—we'll keep it *basic* and pragmatic for our purposes.

One thing we know about the anointing oil—it's a picture of the Holy Spirit's power and it breaks the yoke of bondage (Isaiah 10:27; Zechariah 4:6). When the Spirit's anointed touch is upon what you *have*—your "jar of oil"—He will use it to help you reinvent, break out, and break through to love life!

Again, our working definition for your "jar of oil" includes the special things you *have* that God could, would, or does touch and anoint with His Spirit's power and influence.

In practical terms, we saw this played out in the historical drama *Chariots of Fire* about the 1924 Olympic runner Eric Liddell, who said, "I believe God made me for a purpose, but he also made me fast. And when I run I feel his pleasure."[3] He had the ability to run and God anointed him there. Where do you feel God's pleasure?

It may take some prayerful trial and error to discover what you have and where you feel God's pleasure and anointed touch. Is God's pleasure and anointed touch obvious when you innovate, invest, organize, paint, nurture, care, operate, engineer, sing, speak, create, serve, lead, give, calculate, design, dance, manage, strategize, throw, run? (Get the idea?)

Let's get pragmatic and take inventory of what you *have*. In this chapter, we'll look at your *possessions* and your *quirks*.

## you have possessions

Think about these legendary faith-adventurers of the past. What did God do with what they possessed?

Moses *had* a rod and God touched it to split the Red Sea and deliver His people (Exodus 4:1–2).

The disciples *had* seven loaves of bread and a few fish and Jesus touched them to feed over 4,000 men, as well as women and children (Matthew 15:32–37).

Gideon was told to "go with the strength you *have*" (Judges 6:14 NLT).

God touched and empowered what they had!

In the same way the Maven possessed a little pot of anointing oil, Moses had a rod, the disciples had seven loaves and a few fish, and Gideon had his strength. You, too, possess an *anointed something*, and God wants to touch, multiply, and monetize it to reinvent your life!

Think about your possessions. Let's look at a few practical examples.

**Faith.** Believing God and His Word by faith is one of the most powerful things you can possess! With faith, all things are possible. Never despise the faith you have—even if it's only the size of a mustard seed! What I love about God's economy is the way He levels the playing field for everyone—no matter your background, hometown, or advantage. Jesus said all things are possible to him who believes. Faith gives substance to the things you hope for (Hebrews 11:1 AMPC). I'm not talking about the type of faith that just "wishes upon a star." I'm talking about Bible faith—the type that Jesus said could move mountains and work miracles. The type of faith that takes God at His Word and acts like what He said is true.

If you don't have anything but faith, you have enough for the Lord to touch and multiply!

**Material things.** The Lord can anoint your "stuff" to reinvent your life and livelihood. In a "sharing economy," your material possessions can be God-touched and monetized to help reinvent your life. For example:

- You have a car. You're a good driver. Somebody needs a ride and boom, there's ride sharing.
- You have a vacant house or room. People need a place to stay. Hello rent-a-room!
- You have land, a warehouse, or an office building. People need a place to work. Enter share-your-extra-space!
- You have a closet full of apparel. People need clothes. Introducing online clothing resale opportunities.
- You have money to invest. People need start-up funds for their justice cause or business. Welcome to crowd-sourced funding. (Or, "please-give-me-money, stranger!")

Those are just a few examples of how you can use what you *have* to reinvent! In these peer-to-peer sharing relationships, everyone wins. What *material things* do you have?

**Expertise.** Are you an expert in something? Your expertise may very well be your bottle of "anointing oil" and the key to your reinvention.

You're an expert organizer? Got a knack for business? Golf coach? Cooking instructor? Social media master? Help others and monetize your expertise by sharing your knowledge in how-to videos, a live workshop, online courses, on-demand webinars, conferences, or through some other delivery vehicle.

You're creative and great with graphic design, filmmaking, social media, photography, content writing, or editing? Share

your skill, start a side hustle, or get full-time work through online freelance gigs.

**Hits and misses.** Everything you possess won't be anointed or turn to gold. There's no shame in taking some risks to learn and figure it out. Better to have tried and failed than to not try and regret. I've experienced both hits and misses and so will you.

*This was a hit:* Years ago, as the online learning platforms were becoming popular, I felt a prompting to play with it. I'd written a few books and possessed enough expertise to help an aspiring author self-publish their book, so I developed an online course called "The Inspired Author's Academy," and for a couple of years made it available to would-be authors. It was a fun project! I sensed God's grace as I put it together. Over 200 people signed up for the course, and the most rewarding part was that close to a dozen students wrote and published their first book. In the process, I was able to inspire others and monetize that expertise. As a bonus, I gained an entirely new set of tech skills that still serve me today.

*This was a miss:* After my freshman year in college while trying to earn some extra money over the summer, I'd read about a person who went door to door offering to install peepholes in homeowners' front doors. I thought that sounded easy and fun. (I have no idea why.) So, I went to the hardware store and bought ten peepholes. I found a drill in my mom's garage and off I went to visit my neighbors. I don't know what I was thinking... but who in their right mind would let me drill a hole through their door? I didn't even think about that part. I'm all of eighteen years old and barely knew how to use a drill, but there I go knocking on doors. "Hey, can I drill a hole in your door?" They pretty much answered "No!" I sold exactly zero peepholes! So, there you go... a swing and a miss! (Oh, and there have been plenty of other misses!) It happens to all of us.

What do you have? What's your jar of anointing oil? Where do you sense God's pleasure, prompting, or anointing? What possessions do you have that God could touch and use to help you reinvent?

Not only do you have possessions, but you also have quirks. Let's talk about them.

## you have quirks

We all have quirks and peculiarities! As far as God is concerned, we are all peculiar!

> But you are a chosen generation, a royal priesthood, an holy nation, **a peculiar people**; that you should show forth the praises of him who has called you out of darkness into his marvelous light. (1 Peter 2:9 AKJV)

Robert Fulghum agrees: "We are all a little weird and life's a little weird, and when we find someone whose weirdness is compatible with ours, we join up with them and fall in mutually satisfying weirdness—and call it love—true love."

It's true, we are all *weirdos*—but God wants to use our quirks and unique peculiarities in the reinvention process. Being quirky is a good thing. It's not an excuse for being rude or irresponsible, but it does mean you have permission to not be perfect! One of the core values at our church is, "We're not perfect, but He's not done." It's liberating to own your imperfections and all of your idiosyncrasies.

Your quirks are a part of your story and are often, strangely enough, anointed! What type of quirks and peculiarities do you have?

Let's look at a few stories that will help you identify your own.

**Voices.** If you have a distinct voice, there's a whole market for voice-over people! You may not recognize Arthur Anderson's name, but you probably know his voice! Arthur's peculiar quirk was his ability to imitate voices, and for thirty years he found himself as the voice of the leprechaun for Lucky Charms cereal. Perhaps you remember the famous phrase "Always after me Lucky Charms." His quirky ability to imitate voices allowed him to reinvent his life after he got out of the military.[4]

**Lists.** Maybe you're anointed with a bright mind? Ever heard of Peter Mark Roget? He was an accomplished doctor, lecturer, and inventor. His work influenced the discovery of laughing gas, the creation of the London sewer system, the invention of the slide rule, and the development of the cinema industry. But you probably don't know him for any of those things. When he turned sixty-one and entered his retirement, he went into a depression for about eight years, and during those years, he passed his time making word lists. He categorized words and their meanings. Thousands of them![5]

When he was seventy-three years old, he reinvented his life by putting the 15,000 words he had categorized along with their meanings into a book—what we know today as *Roget's Thesaurus*! *Roget's Thesaurus* has sold upward of thirty-two million copies.[6]

**Awkwardness.** Albert Einstein was a genius. He discovered the law of relativity among many other things. But did you know he had very peculiar idiosyncrasies? He was nonverbal. He didn't speak a word until he was three years old and was socially awkward. Those quirks didn't stop God from touching this man's mind and using him to change the world and help humanity![7]

**Dyslexic.** Leonardo da Vinci was an anointed, left-handed

dyslexic. Being a lefty back in the day wasn't too popular. (As a lefty myself, I have a new appreciation for Leonardo!) Of course, we know him for many things, among them his magnum opus, the *Mona Lisa*.[8]

**Collector.** Years ago, I heard an anecdotal story about an elderly missionary and his wife. They were in their eighties and coming off the mission field, but they'd only saved up $4,000 for their retirement. As they prayed for God's wisdom, the Lord spoke to their heart: "What do you have?" As missionaries, they felt like they didn't have much—well, except their peculiar expertise on collectable Hummel figurines. One of their hobbies on the mission field was to study the Hummel figurine catalog whenever they received one. They didn't recognize this expertise as being of any value, but when they returned to the States, and they were seeking the Lord on what they should do, He led them to put a classified ad in the newspaper (the Craigslist of the day!) that simply said, "We buy Hummels." They did. Lo and behold, people started to contact them, and they bought Hummel figurines from people selling theirs. Once they had spent their $4,000 buying up Hummels, they asked, "Now what, Lord?"

The Lord spoke to their heart: "Put another classified ad in the paper, but this time say, 'We sell Hummels.'" They put an ad in the paper, marked up their price, and sure enough, people started to buy Hummels from them! When they sold all of their Hummels, they said, "Lord, now what?" He said, "Put an ad in the paper that says, 'We buy Hummels.'"

You get the idea?

They bought and sold Hummels for many years. They were so successful they had to rent a warehouse and hire staff to help them! God used a peculiar talent they had and as they followed His guidance, He set them up for their retirement!

What about you? What do you have? When it comes to answering Reinvent Question #2, the Lord will use your *possessions and quirks* to help you reinvent your life!

## reinvention review

1. In what ways does knowing God wants to touch and anoint your *possessions and quirks* inspire you in your own reinvention?
2. When you think about your "jar of anointing oil" in terms of your possessions and quirks, what do you have? List everything you can think of.
3. While it's fresh, write down any ideas for leveraging, monetizing, or utilizing your possessions or peculiar quirks that the Lord has put in your heart.

## chapter 16

# passions and purpose

*It doesn't matter where you come from—what you have, or don't have, what you lack, what you have too much of—but all you need to have is faith in God, an undying passion for what you do, or what you choose to do in this life, and a relentless drive and the will to do whatever it takes to be successful in whatever you put your mind to.*

Stephen Curry

Chick-fil-A was named the number-one fast-food restaurant in America in 2018 and there's a good reason why.[1]

They are passionate about their purpose, and it reflects the Christian faith of its founder, S. Truett Cathy: "To glorify God by being a faithful steward of all that is entrusted to us and to have a positive influence on all who come into contact with Chick-fil-A."

In a world focused on the bottom line, Chick-fil-A sets an example of putting God first and making sure all locations remain closed on Sundays. Their core value of "glorifying God"

has not hurt Chick-fil-A's bottom line. Quite the contrary. God has honored their business practices by allowing them to win awards in setting the standard for customer service among fast-food restaurants.[2]

Chick-fil-A has *passion* and *purpose*—and they've found success.

Let's talk about how this relates to your life as we continue answering Reinvent Question #2.

## reinvent question #2: what do you have?

The Lord will use, touch, and multiply what you *have*. Don't get discouraged by what you don't have—stay focused on what you do have.

The Maven had passion and purpose—to keep her boys and survive! You've also got passions and purpose, and they will be key to your reinvented success.

Let's explore your *passions* and *purpose* and see how God can touch, multiply, and monetize them to reinvent and fulfill your life. I love the way Bishop T. D. Jakes put it in one of his Instagram posts on his account @bishopjakes: "If you can't figure out your purpose, figure out your passion. For your passion will lead you right into your purpose."

Yep. Let's unpack it.

## you have passion

What flips your switch? What do you love? What excites you? What makes you want to get out of bed in the morning? These are good indicators of your passion. Let's look at a few other

ways to identify your passion. How would you answer these questions?

*If money were no object and you were guaranteed success, what would you want to do?*
*If you could only do one thing for the rest of your life, what would it be?*
*What brings you the greatest joy and sense of satisfaction?*
*If you had thirty days of vacation to do whatever you wanted, what would you do?*

Your answers are indicators of your heartfelt—and likely God-given—passion. Let's dig a little deeper by thinking about your passion through various lenses.

**What did you love in third grade?** When you didn't have any responsibilities, pressure, or bills, what did you love to do? When you could do anything you wanted at recess, what did you do? What did you love to do after school or when your homework was done?

Was there anything better than a fresh tub of Play-Doh or a new coloring book? Did you spend hours shaking up your Etch A Sketch, finger painting, or building forts with blankets? Maybe it was plucking around on a piano, playing basketball in the driveway, or playing hide-and-seek with neighbor kids? Maybe you spent your childhood playing video games and writing coding for new apps (kids these days!). I wonder if these third-grade loves are clues to the "jar of anointing oil" God has placed in your life?

When I think about my own life in those elementary years, it seems like I was often writing or creating something! One summer, a few of us put together a backyard carnival and charged the neighbor kids fifty cents to attend. Another year,

my friends and I wrote and performed an original play in our garage. When I reflect back to my younger years, it seems I was always writing a song, a poem, a letter to a friend, or a skit. I liked words. Funny thing, my sisters and I also spent a lot of time playing Mass in the basement, taking turns being "the priest"—passing out the Communion elements or listening to each other's "confessions."

It shouldn't surprise me that God pulled those creative passions together and anointed them in my vocation as a leader, writer, teacher, and pastor. As I've reinvented areas of my life and ministry over the years, I have unknowingly stayed tethered to these passions.

The things you loved in third grade are pointers to the *passions* that are lodged in your heart—this is what you *have*!

**What's your talent stack?** The truth is you likely have more than one passion. In the business world, they call it a "talent stack" and when your passions, experiences, and talents are stacked together, they mean something.

What is your "talent stack"? God's not going to waste any of your talents or experiences. While you may not understand how the various aspects of your life are connected, God has a way of stacking and using them in ways you've not thought of.

I once heard the story of a Christian man who studied French in college and then became an urban developer in the States by trade. He spent most of his life in urban development, but always had a love for France and the French people. In the second half of his life, he felt pulled to do something in ministry, but he had no idea how God could use his "talent stack" of an urban development career with his degree in French. Well, wouldn't you know, God led him to plant churches in France! How perfect is that? He didn't know how his seemingly unrelated passions could come together,

but God always has a way of stacking our talents to reinvent our lives.

Our executive assistant, Tara, is one of those multitalented people who is good at everything. She is putting her talent stack together in a surprising way. In high school she participated in competitive cheerleading, school plays, and band. As a young adult, she went to college to be a teacher and later worked as an administrative assistant to a youth pastor. Now in her thirties, all of these experiences have come together in her role as our executive assistant—while she also volunteers to lead our high school worship team and heads up the performing arts dance team in our church.

God has a way of stacking our talents, reinventing areas of our lives, and causing all things to work together for the good of those who love Him and are called according to His purposes!

**What do you love after forty?** (If you're not there yet, enjoy reading these paragraphs about your future!) It should come as no surprise that our God-given passions will be connected to the things we're interested in—even later in life! It doesn't matter how young or old you are or what your past has looked like. The Lord can use what you have—your passions and interests—to reinvent your life.

Jamal Joseph joined the infamous Black Panther Party in his teens and eventually served ten years in prison. His teen passions did not serve him well, but while in prison, he reinvented his life by cultivating an interest in writing poetry and earning two college degrees. When he was released, he went on to become a successful filmmaker and eventually felt compelled to help young people avoid going down the same road he traveled, so he founded the IMPACT Repertory Theatre of Harlem to keep them off the streets. In addition, he's gone on to write and direct films, teach graduate film courses at Columbia University, and

author several books, including *Panther Baby: A Life of Rebellion and Reinvention.*[3]

At sixty-two years of age, he was awarded the 2015 Purpose Prize, from San Francisco–based nonprofit Encore.org. This award is given to trailblazers over sixty who have tackled social problems creatively and effectively.[4]

I love the story of an older woman who was helping a young Latino man and asked him what he was passionate about and what made him angry. He told her he was passionate about salsa dancing and angry at "old white women" who were disrespectful to him and his friends when they walked down the street. This woman came up with a genius idea to help reinvent this young man's life. She used her interest in dance and helped him stack two of his interests to put together a dance program where he could teach old white women at the community center how to salsa dance—isn't that the best?[5]

Vera Wang wanted to be an Olympic skater. She tried out for the 1968 Olympics and didn't make it. When her dreams of being an Olympian were dashed, it was time to reinvent. She was very interested in fashion and decided to pursue a career with *Vogue* magazine, then with Ralph Lauren and a variety of different designers.[6]

When she was forty years old and about to get married, she commissioned the making of her wedding dress for $10,000. It was a hit! Vera Wang became the "it" fashion designer known for amazing wedding dresses. When her interest in skating didn't pan out, she focused on her interest in fashion and turned it into a lucrative, reinvented career.[7]

At seventy years of age, Bob Becker was the oldest finisher at the 2015 prestigious Badwater Double, a 135-mile run through Death Valley that prides itself as "the world's toughest foot race." He covered the 135-mile course in forty-one hours, thirty

minutes, and twenty-one seconds (that includes 14,600 feet of ascent and extreme heat); then he turned around and threw in an extra eleven-mile run and retraced the 146 miles, making for a round-trip journey of 292 miles. It took him seven days, eight hours, and forty-eight minutes to do it! As an ultra-marathoner, he said, "I'm a little bit unusual at my age, doing these things. I'm told frequently that I inspire a lot of people to get off the sofa and get out there and exercise. And that's a big deal to me."[8]

It's not often you find people over forty years of age in medical school, but Jean Forman knew she always wanted to be a doctor. When all of her children had left for college, it was reinvention time. She wondered what she would do with the rest of her life—she decided to fulfill the dream that wouldn't go away. She completed her ten-year journey to becoming a physician and graduated from USC School of Medicine when she was fifty-one years old. "We each have one lifetime to do something with," she said. "Even if I had not made it to medical school, at least I would know that I tried. If I had not, I would have always wondered, 'What if?' "[9]

I love that: *"I would have always wondered, 'What if?'"* What about you? Do all of these stories stir you up? What *did* you want to be when you grew up? (It's never too late!) What have you always wanted to do? What did you love in third grade? What's your talent stack? What do you love after forty? When you think about these things, in what ways might the Lord want to touch your passions to reinvent your life?

Let's talk about one more thing you *have*!

## you have purpose

You have a divine purpose. God-given potential. Throughout the Bible, He tells us so.

> He has made everything beautiful in its time. He also has planted eternity in men's hearts and minds [**a divinely implanted sense of a purpose** working through the ages which nothing under the sun but God alone can satisfy], yet so that men cannot find out what God has done from the beginning to the end. (Ecclesiastes 3:11 AMPC)

> "For I know **the plans I have for you**," says the LORD. "They are plans for good and not for disaster, to give you a future and a hope." (Jeremiah 29:11 NLT)

Your purpose is a force. It stabilizes, guides, and gives meaning to your life. Purpose is connected to your passion and it's something you *have*! Sometimes you need to discover or rediscover its importance and the way God wants to multiply it! (We'll only scratch the surface here, but if you're interested, I offer an entire online course—*The Inspired Life*—within The Basics University online platform where we go into more detail to help you discover your God-given purpose.[10])

Here are a couple of thoughts to identify and clarify your purpose.

**Your purpose is connected to His cause.** Your purpose will be connected to His cause—and His cause is His church around the world. Jesus *is* building His church—it's the most important thing He is doing on planet earth. When you recognize this (whether you're a teacher, architect, stockbroker, hairstylist, or preacher) and throw your heart, energy, wealth, and time into

helping His cause, you'll experience more fulfillment than you thought possible. In other words, it's not just pastors or missionaries who are called to do kingdom work—as a believer, you are called to further His cause, no matter your vocation. Your *role* in life may be as an engineer, pilot, actor, or grandparent, but your anointed *purpose* in that role is to further His cause and champion His church!

**Your purpose is revealed in His Word.** Although Jesus was fully God and fully man, while operating as a man on earth, He, too, had to discover His purpose as it was revealed in God's Word. Imagine how Jesus felt as a young person (fully God and fully human) when He read Isaiah 61:1–2:

> The Spirit of the Lord GOD is upon Me,
> Because the LORD has anointed Me
> To preach good tidings to the poor;
> He has sent Me to heal the brokenhearted,
> To proclaim liberty to the captives,
> And the opening of the prison to those who are bound;
> To proclaim the acceptable year of the LORD.

As He read the Scriptures, He discovered His purpose and who He was! (In the same way, when we read the Scriptures, we discover our purpose and who we are in Christ! *#truthbomb*)

Jesus embraced His purpose and let the world know Isaiah was being fulfilled through Him when He declared Isaiah 61 in the synagogue (Luke 4).

When it comes to reinventing your life, the best way to discover your purpose is to align with His cause, and the best way to align with His cause is to hear from God through His Word. That's where you'll hear His voice to determine your purpose. Jesus said it best: "It is written, 'Man shall not live by

bread alone, but by every word that proceeds from the mouth of God'" (Matthew 4:4).

What has the Lord spoken to your heart through His Word? Maybe when you were a child? Teen? Adult? What Scriptures have come alive to you? (Jumped off the page, as they say?) When God speaks His Word to your heart, it's alive! His Word gives you purpose, direction, and clarity. You can *literally* live by His Word—it will be an anchor for your soul.

When you embrace the words God speaks to your heart, He causes those very words to become your desire! You will want what He wants—even if at first it was the last thing you thought you wanted!

> For God is working in you, giving you the desire and the power to do what pleases him. (Philippians 2:13 NLT)

As a young man, my husband, Jeff, was a rising star. By eighteen years of age, he had his private, instrument, twin-engine, commercial, and flight instructor ratings in aviation. (He was the youngest flight instructor in the state of Michigan at the time.) He was poised for a career in aviation—that is, until the Vietnam War ended and thousands of jet-rated pilots with thousands of combat flight hours came home to snatch up jobs in the airline industry. Jeff left his dreams of an aviation career and went into business, ultimately becoming a principal partner in a multi-million-dollar commercial lighting agency. He was building a successful business, so he (I mean, *we*!) could have a nice life.

Nine months before we got married, while we were attending a conference and seeking the Lord for our future, the Lord spoke to him from 2 Timothy 2:2: "The things that you have heard from me among many witnesses, commit these to faithful

men who will be able to teach others also." At that time, he knew God's purpose and anointing for him was *not* to build a lighting business, but rather to build a church to bring Jesus, the light of the world, to people in darkness (how cool is that?). God dramatically reinvented his life with purpose to be a pastor—even though it meant a huge pay cut and a drastic lifestyle change.

Although there have been difficult seasons, he's never doubted it nor regretted his decision to follow God's purpose. (Interestingly, the Lord has a way of bringing things full circle and in recent years the Lord has resurrected Jeff's love of flying and opened up new opportunities for him to fly for fun! *#Godisgood*)

**Your purpose is realized as you walk by faith.** Aaron was the district manager overseeing three banking centers in three different cities in Southwest Michigan when the Lord worked a reinvention in his life.

Countless times, he pondered, *What do I want to do with my life?* He was flourishing in the banking world, receiving recognition and honors for his achievements, but he knew there was something else for him.

In 2007, while attending a conference and listening to a leading church organizational consultant, who had been in secular management for a national company, Aaron had a moment. He knew that night he wanted to use his organizational skill set to help our church—either as a volunteer or on staff. That night, Aaron stayed up late praying and pouring out his heart on paper and he sent it to us in an email.

As he prayerfully considered the thought of leaving his ten-year career in the banking industry to follow the purpose and desires God was putting in his heart, a position opened up to oversee our finance department. He knew God was in it and he

joined our staff. Aaron is an exceptional leader and systematic thinker and he's using his gifts to fulfill his purpose.

Today, he serves as an executive pastor and is the director of operations for our ministry! Aaron said:

> When that opportunity was presented to me, I knew that it was where my heart was and the Lord revealed to me that this was the step I needed to take. It's interesting looking back now to realize how big of a step that was for me. But however illogical it may have seemed to leave banking, answering the call to ministry became clear, obvious and exciting.
>
> Since then, I've never grown so much and so consistently personally, mentally, emotionally, and spiritually as I have in these years of being in ministry and walking in God's call for my life. Five years after I started in ministry I stepped into a pastoral role at our church which opened up doors to be used in greater ways than I could have ever imagined. And just as profoundly, walking in His grace at a level that never seemed possible.

What about you? In what ways might the Lord want to reinvent, repurpose, and rearrange your life? When you think about Reinvent Question #2: What do you have?—what are your God-given *passions and purpose*?

## reinvention review

1. What *passions and purpose* did the Lord stir within you as you read this chapter?
2. As it relates to your *passions*, what types of things did you love in third grade? What's your talent stack? What do you love in your over-forty years? (If that fits!) List them.
3. As it relates to your *purpose*, what Scriptures has the Lord spoken to your heart—words you know you are to live by?

## chapter 17

# friends and cronies

*You are the average of the five people you spend the most time with.*

Jim Rohn

I sowed a friendship famine when our kids were preschoolers. I don't recommend it.

I had gotten so busy changing diapers, raising little kids, and helping my husband pioneer our start-up church that I had not made any time for myself or friendships. Being in a new town, being the mom of preschoolers, and being a pastor's wife was the perfect recipe for feeling isolated and alone! As a result, I didn't sow any friendship seeds for several years.

First, I didn't know who to sow them into and second, I didn't make it a priority. Therefore, by the time our baby was turning six months old and our oldest was going into second grade, I realized while I did have a lot of friends at church, on a personal level I had sown a friendship famine. I was lonely.

The only remedy for finding *my people* was to get busy sowing seeds. I knew if I wanted to have friends, I would need to show myself friendly, so I began to strike up conversations with

everyone...cashiers, baristas, teachers, parents, referees, repair techs, the grocery bagger—everyone! I figured by doing this I would find people I clicked with and then I'd start sowing a few extra seeds into those relationships. Sowing friendship seeds worked! It didn't take long before several life-giving friendships began to sprout and a new season of heartfelt friendship blossomed.

We can avoid friendship famines by being intentional to sow into our relationships. Jesus told us to "love others as well as you love yourself." When it comes to reinventing your life, people are going to be a big part of it, so let's sow some seeds!

When you think about what you *have*, have you thought about your friendships? Your friends and cronies are a big part of reinventing your life. Let's carry on with this discussion as we continue answering Reinvent Question #2.

## reinvent question #2: what do you have?

What do you have—or better yet, "who" do you have? You have people—specifically, friends! God will use the people in your world to help reinvent your life and He'll use you in theirs, too. Think about the Maven. She had *troublemakers* and *rainmakers* in her life! The creditors created the turmoil as they threatened to take her kids, but God positioned Elisha in her life to be a source of divine help, just when she needed it.

It's definitely better to have friendly rainmakers, rather than troublemakers! Who has the Lord positioned in your life?

## your tribe

We all belong to various groups, communities, spheres, or tribes of people. In 1990, Robin Dunbar, anthropologist and professor emeritus of evolutionary psychology at the University of Oxford, came to the conclusion that as humans, our brains have the capacity to engage and connect with an average of 150 people in a stable and meaningful way. This is known as the Dunbar Number.[1]

Not everyone agrees with the Dunbar Number theory; other studies with different parameters have concluded the average person's network capacity could be anywhere between 400 and 600 people. No need to debate it—for our purposes, let's agree most of us have a few hundred people in our "tribe," and we are connected to these people at some meaningful level.

How does knowing this help you reinvent your life? When you realize the people in your life are a gift and a precious resource—both personally and professionally—you get more focused on loving, nurturing, serving, and caring about them.

Let's look at a breakdown of the various groups of people in your life.

**Very close friends.** A small group of very close friends would be under fifteen people. These are those closest to you—your family (we'll get to them next), your very best friends, people you would confide in. These are the ones who would sit with you in the emergency room. Who is on your short list of very close friends?

**Close friends.** Your close friends would be fifty or so people. These are the people you'd enjoy going on vacation with, having over for a dinner party, or sitting in the bleachers with at a sporting event. In other words, you like to hang out with the

people in this group. Who are your close friends? Who are you inviting over for dinner and a table games night?

**Important friends—your Dunbar Number.** The Dunbar Number represents around 150 friends. These are people you'd consider to be important friends. You have the capacity and desire to share your time, energy, support, conversation, and life with these friends. Who's on your list? A good way to determine your "Dunbar Number" is to ask yourself who you'd invite to an important event like a private party or your son or daughter's wedding. Those are your important friends. (*Not* that *everyone* isn't important...jeepers!)

**Casual acquaintances.** This is a larger group, even up to 500. You may not know everyone's name in this group, but you remember how or where you met them. High school friends. College alumni. Coworkers. Neighbors. Church friends. You are glad to have their acquaintance.

**Network of people.** This is your larger network of people upward of 1,500 and would be made up of your large group associations and social media connections.

People can move in and out of these various circles, but once you identify the people in your various spheres, think about ways to nurture the relationships you want to blossom. Let's take a moment to focus on cultivating, and even reinventing, friendships.

## reinvent your everyday friendships

I love these stories from *Reader's Digest*. They are heartwarming and a good reminder to sow friendship seeds into our everyday friendships.

Shannon, my best friend of over twenty-six years, and I text each other every morning with "Good morning, beautiful!" or "Hello, gorgeous!" That way, we both start the day with a smile.

—Katrina La Force, Petaluma, California

After my wife of forty-four years died, I didn't feel the urge to socialize. But that didn't stop my friend Tony from inviting me to join a group of guys who got together every Thursday for dinner. I told him I wasn't ready. He called again the next week, and again I said no. He kept calling every week, and finally I said, "OK, I'll go. Anything to keep you from calling me every week." It has now been six years since my wife died, and thanks to Tony, I have been going to dinner every week with the gang we've dubbed ROMEO—Retired Old Men Eating Out.

—David Fenwick, Ocean Township, New Jersey

Today is my birthday, and I know my friend Linda is making me a cake. Sometimes when you're an adult, no one thinks to do that for you.

—Tamara Castellari, Parachute, Colorado[2]

Sowing seeds into friendships takes effort and patience, but it is rewarding. Friendships take time and require an investment of communication, initiative, and intentionality. If your friendships are suffering or seasons have changed, this is a great time to reinvent and sow some fresh seeds. Maybe it's a phone call? Sending a funny text? An invitation to coffee or dinner. Go ahead and sow, baby, sow! If you sow, you will reap.

Let's get more specific. Prayerfully consider sowing into these friendships...

**Old friends.** The good news is that you have "old friends"! These are your cronies! Reconnecting with old friends is a good place to sow and a great way to reinvent your friendship life. The history you share means something. The inside jokes. These things often make picking up where you left off easy. Any Girl Scouts out there? We used to sing it around the campfire: "Make new friends, but keep the old. One is silver and the other gold." It was through one of my grade-school Brownie troop friends, Andrea, that I came to know the Lord. I'm so glad I *had* that friendship and eternally grateful she led me to the Lord. Maybe you're supposed to be an Andrea for someone?

**Work, neighbor, and bleacher friends.** I know several people who've found their best friends in the bleachers, down the street, or in the next cubicle! Maybe you regularly bump into someone who loves to hike? Ride a bike? Play pickleball? Shop the outlet mall? Visit over coffee? Eat toffee? (Sheesh! I'm starting to feel like Dr. Seuss over here.) Take the initiative to get that friendship going.

**Game night friends.** When our kids graduated from high school and we entered the empty-nest season, we didn't see our "bleacher buddies" as much, so we had to reinvent our friendships. We decided to start some new traditions. We like to throw a party, so we invited three couples over for a bring-a-semi-gourmet-dish-to-pass dinner and night of playing cards. It was a blast and we decided to rotate houses and do it once a month. Here we are more than six years later and still having a good time. Our friendships have deepened; we've laughed, cried, and shared weddings, baby showers, and funerals with one another. We've vacationed together and developed many inside jokes along the way. Nurturing friendships is worth every seed sown. If you're anointed to eat and have fun, throw a party and start some new friendships! (High fives all around!)

**Prayer and Bible study friends.** There's nothing like praying with friends. When our kids were in school, I really enjoyed being in a Moms in Touch prayer group with three other moms. Our hearts were connected in that season as we prayed specific prayers for each other's kids and saw the Lord answer those prayers. The friendships in that season were equally rewarding. If you get excited about that type of thing, ask around and see if there is a prayer group you could be a part of.

**Long-distance friends.** Depending on your location and line of work, you may need to cultivate long-distance friends. Many missionaries and pastors we know cultivate friendships with church leaders in other parts of the world. Technology definitely helps! Jeff and I enjoy trading encouragement and ideas with our ministry friends and I am personally refreshed by exchanging texts and social media messages with my pastor gal pals in other parts of the world. My friend Tori and her sister Beth keep in touch by talking on the phone *every* day! My friend Beth (a different one and apparently a popular name in this paragraph!) and I send each other random emoticons at random times for the sole reason of bringing each other a random smile. And at least once a week, often on a Monday, my friend Wendy and I send a fun meme, a heartfelt text, or video chat to update on life. It's refreshing!

So, figure out what works for you and sow those friendship seeds.

**Online friends.** It's not a new thought, but you can make friends online! Sure, there are dating apps for singles and social media apps for everyone, and if you'll be wise, authentic, and God-honoring in your use of online opportunities, you can make some Insta-besties! (Shout-out to mine! One day we'll get to have a long chat over coffee!!) Find a community online where you're encouraged in your journey and sow some cheer into the lives of those you meet.

In addition to the friendships we have in our day-to-day lives, there are other God-knit friendships to steward.

### reinvent your god-knit friendships

A friend who impacted my life put it this way: "God always leads us to people who lead us to Him." It's true. There is nothing better than God-knit friendships—whether for a reason, a season, or a lifetime—that encourage, lift, and cheer you on in your God-given potential. Do you need to reinvent your relationships among Jesus lovers? You can. Here are a couple of ways to cultivate those kinds of friendships:

**Be encouraging.** After a particularly difficult season, I received a note from a pastor friend with *eight anointed words*. He said, "My wife and I are in your corner." I cried. As a woman, co-leading our church with my husband and preaching 50 percent of the time on Sunday mornings, I had received my share of "We don't believe in women pastors—why does she speak?" comments, so when I got his encouraging note, I can't tell you how life-giving those anointed words were to my heart.

The truth is, everyone needs words like these. What's the nicest thing anyone's ever said about you? What anointed, life-giving words could you share with someone who needs them? Maybe it's not words—maybe it's a hug, or a few hours cleaning their house, or an unexpected gift, or a couple of hours to talk. It's surprising how God anoints *encouragement* to reinvent God-knit friendships.

**Be interested.** Dale Carnegie's ageless advice still holds true and is worth repeating: "To be interesting, be interested."

Asking questions is the key here. Your questions show your interest. Nothing is worse than a one-way conversation or

relationship. When you are interested in others, questions come easily because you want to know about them. A good friend will return the favor and show interest in your life by asking questions, too.

Someone once said, "Check on your strong friend." Maybe you know someone who looks like they always have it together, but the truth is they could use an encouraging phone call and some interest from a friend. Be interested!

**Invite people into your circle.** It's terrible to feel out of place as an awkward, uninvited outsider—whether it's at a work event, a neighborhood party, church, or some other gathering. You can only shuffle your feet, pretend to look for something in your purse, or check your phone so many times. (Not that I have ever done this before.) So, next time you see an awkward soul in your social circles, help a bro or sis out. Show interest—ask them a question! Any question—they'll tell you anything, while secretly thinking, *Please, just don't leave me! #iwillgiveyouallmypasswords*

**Be sweet with your words.** Anyone else have cringeworthy gaps in this department? I grew up in an era of straight shooters. They didn't try to hide what they meant. Whether it was family, friends, teachers, or preachers—their words were direct, honest, and heartfelt. I knew they loved me, and while their words were helpful, they were not always loaded with grace. I inadvertently adopted the same style and didn't think twice about it until I heard myself and realized I needed some reinvention. I knew my heart motivation was pure, but I could tell my words needed seasoning with more grace. For the past many years, I've been praying for the Lord to help me talk, write, and teach more like what is described in Proverbs 16:21–24 (TPT). Anyone want to join me?

The one with a wise heart is called "discerning,"
and **speaking sweetly to others**
**makes your teaching even more convincing.**
Wisdom is a deep well of understanding
opened up within you as a fountain of life for others,
but it's senseless to try to instruct a fool.
Winsome words pour from a heart of wisdom,
adding value to all you teach.
**Nothing is more appealing**
**than speaking beautiful, life-giving words.**
For they release sweetness to our souls
and inner healing to our spirits.

Maybe you're looking for God-knit friends? The Lord has a way of leading us to people who lead us to Him—so pray and trust Him to help you in this area. A good starting spot is your local church. If you have one, get planted and plug in. If you don't have one, this weekend is the perfect time to take a risk and visit a few. The Lord will order your steps to divine friendships and He'll reinvent this area of your life.

When you think about Reinvent Question #2: What do you have?—remember, He's going to use your *friends and cronies* to help you reinvent.

## reinvention review

1. How does thinking about your *friends and cronies* encourage you to reinvent your life?
2. If you were to write down your Dunbar List of "important friends," which 150 people would make your list? (Whose Dunbar List would you be on?)
3. What three ways can you sow friendship seeds into the people in your world this week?

# chapter 18

# family and kinfolk

*People are basically the same the world over. Everybody wants the same things—to be happy, to be healthy, to be at least reasonably prosperous, and to be secure. They want friends, peace of mind, good family relationships, and hope that tomorrow is going to be even better than today.*

Zig Ziglar

Okay, who else's family goes bonks at the wedding reception when the DJ busts out Sister Sledge and "We Are Family"? Yep, ours does, too. Every time. With fourteen nieces and nephews between all my sisters and me, there have been a lot of weddings, and as soon as we hear the first note of the song—you know it—all of us, the bride, the groom, the in-laws, the out-laws, and the whole family are up on our feet busting a move on the dance floor. *#heyhey*

There's just something about family. No matter how functional or dysfunctional, innately we want to embrace that sentiment—"we are family"—if only for a few minutes on the dance floor. And, the truth is, the cure for much of the pain in your life—isolation, loneliness, and feeling unimportant—

can be found as you allow the Lord to touch what you have: your family.

Let's return to the Maven's story and continue looking at Reinvent Question #2.

**reinvent question #2: what do you have?**

Interestingly, when Elisha asked the Maven what she had, he specifically said, "Tell me, what do you have in the *house*?" (2 Kings 4:2). Maybe there's a nuance there and in answering this question, we need to ask, "*Who* do we have in the *house*?" We have people in our house. Our family! Our kinfolk!

When it comes to family, you may feel *warm fuzzies* or you may feel *cold pricklies*.

It's possible you were raised in a traditional, two-parent home and life was grand. Your family is intact and, other than normal idiosyncrasies, you love each other and it's all good in your hood. That is awesome, by the way!

Or perhaps, like me, you came from a broken home—or worse, an abusive home—and that has impacted you greatly. Maybe you're an adult who was on the receiving end of a divorce you didn't ask for and your heart is broken. I'm sorry you didn't get what you deserved in a loving home. I understand.

Or maybe your parents stayed together, but your dad was abusive and your mom was an alcoholic—and you were lost in the shuffle. It's possible your princess sister or perfect brother got all the love, while you were stuck "in your own little corner, in your own little chair" trying to make sense of this thing called family. (Family pain is complex on many levels and it wouldn't hurt to visit with a Christian family counselor to work through some things, if you are struggling.)

Family is God's idea and insomuch as you are able and as people are willing, God wants to touch, restore, reset, refresh, and reinvent your family relationships. Let's look at these relationships:

*Your relationship with your spouse.*
*Your relationship with your kids.*
*Your relationship with your parents.*

Your time, money, and energy cannot be spent on anyone, anywhere, any better.

## reinvent your relationship with your spouse

There are many exceptional resources on marriage, so I'll share just a few practical nuggets that have helped me and my husband enjoy over thirty years of marriage. Perhaps a few of these will help you to recalibrate your marriage.

**Keep Jesus at the center.** You are in a love triangle! When Jesus stays at the top of the triangle, the closer each of you get to Him, the closer you automatically get to one another. When Jesus satisfies your heart and you are complete in Him, you release your spouse from the unrealistic need to be your all-in-all. (Plus, you don't go searching for love in all the wrong places.) When Jesus is at the center of your marriage, His love fills your heart in a real way and you are free to enjoy your spouse. So, the best thing you can do to improve your marriage today? Put Jesus where He belongs—in the center of your life and marriage. (Amen. Hallelujah. Preach it, sister.)

**Laugh about all of it.** For sure! Life is hard. Busy. Unpredictable. Laugh anyway. In the same day, your spouse will be

amazing and they will let you down. In the same breath, they'll say something brilliant and hurtful (or use the wrong tone, I've heard). There are highs and lows in marriage. There are highs and lows in life. Fix what you can and laugh off the rest. (Or...be a frustrated, angry, and miserable human being to live with. Your choice. *Smile.*)

**Learn their love language.** In theory this is great. Yes, you should *learn* your spouse's love language. The problem is, it's hard to *speak* it. My husband is an "acts of service" and "physical touch" love language guy and I'm a "words of affirmation" and "gifts" gal. He touches and serves the heck out of me...and even though it's not my language, I know he loves me. I talk his ear off and buy him clothes he never wears. He knows I love him. (If you've never read *The 5 Love Languages* by Gary Chapman, I highly recommend reading it...and putting it into practice is even better!)

**Enjoy what they enjoy.** It's not the exotic trips or obligatory anniversary celebrations; it's the daily stuff. So, figure out what your spouse enjoys and enjoy it together. (I know what you're thinking and yes, *that*, too, but there are other things in married life! *#eyeroll*) In our empty-nest season, my husband and I are finding a new rhythm. We both enjoy golfing, so Friday morning golf dates have become a fun tradition. We like short mystery trips to find greasy little out-of-the-way breakfast diners, so we hop in the car and search. We like late-night pontoon rides where we can dance in the moonlight to the classic "Unchained Melody" and I can sing off-key in his ear. What does your spouse enjoy? Start reinventing your marriage today by planning a date where you do what they enjoy doing!

These are just a few ideas to get your wheels spinning and remind you there are lots of ways to reinvent your relationship with your spouse. No matter where your marriage is, you can

ask God for the customized ideas you need. (Not trying to be too deep here, but if your marriage is in trouble and you need the big guns to help you reinvent it, as previously mentioned, by all means seek out qualified Christian counselors to help you.)

### reinvent your relationship with your kids

Whether you have given birth to, adopted, or fostered your children, what an amazing honor to be entrusted with the stewardship of caring for, guiding, and raising your children for the Lord—helping them to become "independently dependent upon Him" before they leave your nest!

Everyone tells you raising kids is a blink. As one person put it, "the days are long, but the years are short." Boy, is it ever true. If you still have kids at home—on top of being their twenty-four-hour butler, chauffeur, maid, and banker—perhaps, it would be good to refresh your relationships with them? And if your kids have long since moved out of the house, it's possible to reinvent your relationship with your adult kids and grands, too.

People have asked us what types of things we did to nurture our family and raise "Christian" kids. We've all heard stories about "those pastors' kids," so I am always cautious when sharing these things. Every family is different, and we'll be the first to tell you our family is not perfect. To be honest, as our kids were growing up, we rarely preached sermons on parenting because we did not know if the way we were doing it was actually working! (Hate to have people trying to *keep up with the Joneses* until we knew our methods worked. Ha.) In recent years, by God's grace, we can see the fruit and the verdict is in—our methods worked!! Our kids turned out to be great people, now married to our fave "in-loves" (Brodie, Zack, Kelsey, and Alexa), all living

for the Lord and starting to pop out babies. So, whether you're raising a millennial, a Gen Zer, or an Alpha kid, here are a few random things I hope inspire you to reinvent your relationship with your kids.

**Pray.** Every parent already knows this. This is definitely the number one thing I did. Hands down. Praying God's Word over your kids is the most important, anointed, and eternal thing you can do for them. We regularly prayed the prayers in Ephesians 1:14–20, Ephesians 3:14–20, and Colossians 1:9–12, among others, over them. Praying for and declaring His protection over them is another biggie. We said these words over them often: "The Name of Jesus, the blood of Jesus and the angels of God surround you and protect you everywhere you go—front to back, side to side, top to bottom—spirit, soul, and body." (Our worship team even wrote a song about it called "Surrounded." Give it a listen and sing it over your family!)[1]

**Hugs and "I love yous."** Whether being touchy-feely comes naturally to you or not, your kids need hugs, back rubs, hand holding, and lots of "I love yous." If it's not your norm already, just start and don't stop! You'll create a loving culture in your family. These days, it's rare that we leave each other's company—even now that they are grown and married—without a hug and an "I love you."

**Be a team.** There's something about developing your family culture—establishing traditions, sharing funny text threads, or creating your own theme song. In our case, we were Team Jones in motion, and for many years we went everywhere (church, sports practice, games, grocery shopping, you name it!) together as a family. It gave our kids security and a solid identity. We didn't allow lone rangers. We'd seen a few families where one of the kids went rogue, isolated themselves, and became the black sheep of the family. It was really sad to watch and it's a hard thing

to turn around. So, we didn't allow it—when one of the kids pulled away, was down, or having a bad attitude, we had a lot of strategies to bring them back to the fold with a good attitude.

**Get them talking.** Relationships are built upon words. Taking advantage of talks in the car, in the kitchen, before bed, anytime we could get a good conversation going, we jumped on it—nonchalantly, of course, as if it's not a big deal. (The kids smell parental overkill a mile away.) A good decoy is to take them to dinner, a football game, a concert, even coffee before school—"when you're buying, their words are flying!" It's important to be intentional in asking good questions—the kind they might want to answer. Questions like, "Tell me the three best and worst things about school today," versus "How was school today?" Or "Who are your two favorite people to follow on Instagram or YouTube?" versus "Do you have any bad friends on Facebook?" These are your conversation starters and before you know it, they're spilling the beans on the things you really want to know.

**Make fun memories.** You only have them under your roof for a few short years, so make sure it's memorable. Be less serious. More fun. Encourage them to skip school with you at least once ~~a week~~. Take vacations. Make long trips in the SUV so they can spill pop and fight...and so you can watch *Frozen* again and again. (Just cracking myself up over here!) Buy roadside cherries and spit pits out the window. Play poker with licorice and Smarties. Relive your favorite memories, like, "Remember the time Luke made us all stop laughing because he was afraid he would actually 'die of laughing'?" And "Remember the time Eric put on all of his Chicago Bears apparel and wouldn't let us talk on Super Bowl Sunday, because *he* had to focus and get ready for the big game?" And "Remember the time Mom went ballistic..." (Whoa. Whoa. That's enough.)

**Give them a spiritual foundation.** Find time to impart God's Word into their lives. It's not easy with busy schedules, but it is really important. My husband opened up "Big Daddy's Bistro" in our kitchen every morning at 7:00 a.m. Before school, he made the kids a hot breakfast and had a Bible devotional time with them. I thought then (and still believe) that was a hugely anointed thing for him to do. The memory of that time with their dad and the living example of their Heavenly Father's consistency is priceless.

When our kids were teenagers and asking "tough" questions about God, the Bible, and cultural topics, we felt prompted to have a few "Kick Butt Theology Nights" where the kids brought their Bibles and a notebook and as a family we got into the Word to find God's answers to the various questions they had. (This was before Google!) We wanted them to see what God said in black and white in their own Bibles—and we wanted to teach them how to let the Bible interpret itself, rather than relying on a commentator or opinionated classmate! It was always enlightening.

**Remove the pressure.** Set the bar where God sets it. We told our kids we didn't have to live up to anyone's expectations, just God's. (As if!) All the Lord asked us to do was to "be Christians" and "live a life pleasing to Him." That meant there were expectations but also loads of grace. In addition, I believe the Lord gave me a good nugget when our kids were entering middle school. He reminded me that Jesus was the only perfect person and our kids would make mistakes (no surprise), and He helped me set our expectation in the right place by encouraging me to "pray their mistakes are minor and that they learn quickly." So that's what we did and that's what they did.

**Make church a priority.** In a post-Christian world that spends more time online than in person, get your family in

church. When our kids were growing up, we went to church every Sunday and we were in all four services (okay, well, we pastored the church, but still). As parents, you have to model love for God, His church, serving others, giving sacrificially, and sharing the gospel. Online services, podcasts, and live streaming are great—we offer all of it—but there is something in God's heart about "not forsaking the assembling of ourselves together" (Hebrews 10:25). Going to church together as a family will mark your kids for a lifetime. As the parent, you set the example.

### reinvent your relationship with your parents

Let's wrap up by talking about a special group of people—our parents.

The Lord has a lot to say about the way we treat our parents—birth parents, adoptive parents, foster parents, and stepparents. Honor is one thing we can give them, and it comes with a two-fold promise, that it would go well with us and we would live long on the earth.

> "Honor your father and mother," which is the first commandment with promise: "that it **may be well with you** and you **may live long on the earth**." (Ephesians 6:2–3)

In what ways could and should you honor your parents? Do they have a big anniversary coming up? Is there a "dream trip" you could take them on? How about updating their home or paying off their house? Buying them a car or motorized scooter? Could you send them a thoughtful note? Invite them over for a home-cooked meal? Take them out for ice cream? A friend of

mine has committed to playing cards with her aging dad every Wednesday night.

I love what two friends of ours, Pastors Mark and Kim Pothier (aka Real Talk Kim), did to honor their parents. As they prepared to get married, they assumed they'd live in San Diego until they asked the Lord what He wanted. Immediately, He spoke to their hearts and told them to set aside their own ministry ambitions, sell everything they had, and move to Fayetteville, Georgia, to serve Kim's parents.

So, on their wedding day, they moved from San Diego to Georgia to do just that! Mark left California, the place he'd called home for fifty years, his business of thirty-six years, and a $3,000-a-week paycheck to assist Kim's dad as the executive pastor of Church of the Harvest for $500 a week (that was a $130,000 annual pay cut!). Mark said, "It was the best move I ever made. Along with Kim, I gained two best friends (Kim's parents) and today we are continuing their legacy." Overnight, the church grew from 50 to 500!

Today, Mark serves as the senior pastor and the church is thriving. On top of that, Kim's traveling ministry and social media presence has mushroomed, as she's keeping it real for almost one million followers on Instagram—encouraging them to get serious about their walk with God. Mark said, "I believe with all my heart that God honors honor!" (Amen!)

My sisters and I tried to honor our parents in big and little ways. My dad always wanted to go on a cruise with his four daughters, so when he turned sixty-five, we took him, and he loved every minute. My full-blooded Irish mother's dream was to go to Ireland, so when she turned seventy, my sisters and I took her to the Emerald Island. Honoring them in those ways has given all of us meaningful memories.

In my mother's last few years, our youngest sister, Michelle,

and her husband, Craig, opened up their home to care for Mom. It sounds great in theory and it was an incredible gift to give her—but it wasn't easy. It was honor. *#honorainteasy* They have some funny stories and no regrets now that Mom is in heaven.

Perhaps the idea of honoring your parents, one or both of them, seems like it's in a galaxy far away due to the deep wounds and hurts lodged in your heart. But rather than dwelling in a place of hurt or living with an "orphan spirit," you can make the choice to reinvent your life in this area. Knowing God's tender love for you, choose to forgive them and then look for ways to honor them. To forgive doesn't mean you approve of or agree with what happened or how you were treated, but it does mean you are willing to let God's love enter in and not hold it against them any longer. Forgiveness opens the door for the Lord to reinvent something within your own heart.

Maybe start by writing a tribute to honor your parents. What would you say?

When it comes to Reinvent Question #2: What do you have?—cultivating our relationships with *family and kinfolk* is important. Family is the Lord's specialty. He'll guide you.

We've covered a lot in all of the chapters dedicated to answering Reinvent Question #2: What do you have? While the Maven had a jar of anointing oil, I hope you've realized all the "jars of anointing oil" you have in your possession, as well as the quirks, passions, purpose, friends, cronies, family, and kinfolk! In the same way God touched and multiplied the Maven's oil, no doubt He'll touch and multiply what you have. Now, let's jump into Reinvent Question #3.

## reinvention review

1. How does thinking about reinventing your relationships with your *family and kinfolk* help and challenge you?
2. How can you sow into your marriage, spouse, family, and kids' lives?
3. In what ways can you honor your parents—whether living or gone?

section 7

# reinvent question #3: *what will you do?*

# chapter 19

# go, get this party started

> *Do the one thing you think you cannot do. Fail at it. Try again. Do better the second time. The only people who never tumble are those who never mount the high wire. This is your moment. Own it.*
>
> Oprah Winfrey

In 2001, my husband ran the Chicago Marathon. When it was *go* time, the starting line was electric as some 30,000 runners lined up to run their race—I've never seen so many physically fit people in one place! My four kids and I "ran" too—from Starbucks to Starbucks as we cheered him on at various mile markers along the way. After several hours, we made our way to the finish line and cheered for him as he finished the race.

At the finish line of the Chicago Marathon, it didn't matter *how* the runners finished—only *that* they finished! They got a medal. They took the photo. They could tell their grandkids! I can't say that. I can say I drank several cappuccinos while my husband ran the Chicago Marathon but the fruit of finishing the race is his to enjoy!

Runners of all ages, shapes, and sizes crossed the finish line.

It was fun to watch! Some got a jolt of energy to finish and then collapsed; others came limping, staggering, crawling, and fighting across. But they finished!

Here's the thing about the Chicago Marathon, or any race: You can't finish if you don't start. The same thing is true when reinventing your life. God can't help you finish until you get started! Let's revisit the Maven to see how this played out in her story as we answer Reinvent Question #3: What will you do? Over the next several chapters, let's look at the specific things we can do to reinvent our lives:

Go, Get This Party Started
Borrow, Baby, Borrow
Shut the Door and Pour
Ring the Bell and Sell

### reinvent question #3: what will you do?

Then he said, "**Go, borrow** vessels from everywhere, from all your neighbors—empty vessels; do not gather just a few. And when you have come in, you shall shut the door behind you and your sons; then **pour** it into all those vessels, and set aside the full ones."

So she went from him and shut the door behind her and her sons, who brought the vessels to her; and she poured it out. Now it came to pass, when the vessels were full, that she said to her son, "Bring me another vessel."

And he said to her, "There is not another vessel." So the oil ceased. Then she came and told the man of God. And he said, "Go, **sell** the oil." (2 Kings 4:3–7)

What will *you* do? Notice four key action words in the Maven's reinvention: *go*, *borrow*, *pour*, and *sell*. These four words provide us with big markers in developing our reinvention roadmap and game plan. These four words—the "to dos"—give us a practical, step-by-step system for reinventing our lives, so let's spend the next four chapters focused on it!

## go, the light is green!

Let's start with "go"! When it comes to solving the Maven's crisis, she was told to "go" launch a business! Keep in mind, up until this point we have no record of her being an entrepreneur or businesswoman. For all we know, she's been a stay-at-home mom loving her kids and supporting her husband. When she found herself at the reinvention crossroads with big gaps between her *ideal* life and her *real* life, this was no time to make excuses, minimize herself, or apologize for her lack of workplace experience—this was her time to obey God and "fake it until you make it" as she got *going* to launch some type of sales career!

Maybe you can relate? No matter how inexperienced or terrified you feel as you reinvent areas in your life, you can push past inertia and fear and *go*!

I love the simple encouragement in this post circulating around Instagram:

Start by doing 1 push-up
Start by drinking 1 cup of water
Start by paying toward 1 debt
Start by reading 1 page
Start by making 1 sale

Start by deleting 1 old contact
Start by walking 1 lap
Start by attending 1 event
Start by writing 1 paragraph
Start today
Repeat tomorrow

Go! That means get off the couch. Get in motion. Get moving. Start. Take some steps. You've got to move it, move it! You've heard it said, "God can't direct a parked car." That's true, but when you put it in drive, remember you don't have to go 100 miles an hour. You can go 5 miles an hour and see how and where He leads you. It doesn't matter where you're at in life. You are not too young, and you are not too old—you can go! The light is green and you can get started.

Think about Julia Hawkins; like a hurricane, she got going and made history at 103 years of age:

> Julia "Hurricane" Hawkins didn't start her running career until she was 100 years old. She thought it would be fun to run the 100-yard dash at 100. In 2019, at 103 years old she broke the record as the oldest runner for the 50 and 100 meter runs in the National Senior Games in Albuquerque, New Mexico. She hopes to inspire others that "you can still be doing it at this kind of age."[1]

Ben Carson said it well: "You have the ability to choose which way you want to go. You have to believe great things are going to happen in your life. Do everything you can—prepare, pray, and achieve—to make it happen."[2]

Jesus said:

> "All authority has been given to Me in heaven and on earth. **Go therefore** and make disciples of all the nations, baptizing them in the name of the Father and of the Son and of the Holy Spirit, teaching them to observe all things that I have commanded you; and lo, I am with you always, even to the end of the age." Amen. (Matthew 28:18–20)

Jesus gave us the emphatic green light to *go* into all the world to make disciples! In general, in addition to going to fulfill the Great Commission, you can infer that you have a green light to *go* ahead and pursue what the Lord has put in your heart.

The first words the apostle Paul received after his conversion were "Arise and **go** into the city, and you will be told what you must do" (Acts 9:6). It wasn't a lot of information, but it was specific, and it was enough.

"Go into the city"—that's all the direction he got. So, he had to *go* with what he had. (And so do we!) That's how the Lord works. That's how reinvention works. God will give you enough information to *go* and take the next step. He does not usually give you the whole map, a twelve-page business plan, or thirty-two studies on the pros and cons. He just says, "Go!" When you take the specific step He gives, like "go into the city," He gives you more direction. Keep in mind, the Maven didn't get the whole plan, either. She had to "go" by faith and trust God for every step.

Let's look at a few practical ways to "go" and reinvent your life.

### go do something every day

First, pray. If you'll *go* to God in prayer, you'll receive His wisdom, strategies, and insights. Prayer gives you an advantage!

In addition to prayer, *go* do something **every day**!

Eleanor Roosevelt said, "Do one thing every day that scares you."

Bob Goff, a self-proclaimed "recovering lawyer" and author of *Love Does*, quits something every Thursday! "Change can be good," Bob says. "[Quitting] frees you up and it works. It's not for everybody. It might drive you crazy, and if that's the case, don't do it." The idea is to quit things that hold you back from other more important things.[3]

Casey Neistat, a YouTuber with two billion views (big!) makes and posts one video every day (small!).[4]

James Altucher, author of *Reinvent You*, writes down ten ideas every day so at the end of the year, he has 3,650 ideas!

What are you willing to do every day?[5]

Warren Buffett was asked, "What is the secret to your success?" He pointed to a stack of books and said, "Read 500 pages a day. That's how knowledge works. It builds up like compound interest."[6]

What if you set a goal to *go* ahead and read a book a week this year? If you don't want to read a whole book, I've enjoyed using getAbstract and Blinkist, two great apps that help me read or listen to hundreds of book abstract summaries in ten minutes or less.

I love what my friend Nicole is doing. She made a list of twenty things she wants to start doing this year. From reading a book a month to practicing her French-speaking skills, to eating less sugar; rather than feeling overwhelmed and trying to do them all at once, she's focusing on one or two new habits each month. She said, "I know myself well enough that trying to do all twenty things at the same time would be overwhelming and I know as soon as I'd drop the ball on one, I'd get discouraged and quit working on the rest." The cool thing is how Nicole

is building on her successes each month by "snowballing" last month's habits into the new monthly habits she's working on. Brilliant!

I recently heard about Pastor Doug, who makes it his goal to pray for someone every day! Not in his *official role as a pastor*, but in his *official role as a Christian*. He looks for God-opportunities to pray for people throughout his day. He said when you connect people to the grace of God with a few kind words and a prayer, "life gets very exciting and the stories are endless! There's a sense of fulfillment in being involved in what God is doing in people's lives on a day-to-day basis." *#goals*

## go with style like my friend kyle

Let me tell you about my friend Kyle.

Kyle is one of my favorite twenty-six-year-olds: He's a humble, gifted filmmaker, and one of the nicest, most unassuming young men you'll ever meet. During his day job, he's the senior video editor for *The Basics With Beth* TV program and pours his heart into his work. During the rest of his time, he's on the *go*, putting his heart and soul into several other things every day.

Kyle's dream is to be a filmmaker, so rather than *waiting* for that to just happen, Kyle is *going* for it by throwing himself into Throwback Pictures, a film company he started. He's already made several full-length and short films and has actors like Creed Bratton (*The Office*), Carel Struycken (*The Addams Family*), Richard Riehle (*Office Space*), Lester Speight (*Transformers: Dark of the Moon*), Larry Hankin (*Home Alone*), Jeffrey Weissman (*Back to the Future II* and *III*), and Trevor Snarr (*Napoleon Dynamite*) starring in his films.

Kyle's been honing his craft since high school, when he started

sending letters to actors and moviemakers to let them know how much he admired them. (A number of these celebrities sent back letters and signed photographs. Some of his favorite autographed responses have come from Michael J. Fox, Robin Williams, and Henry Winkler.) He sent letters to thirty different directors and producers in Hollywood introducing himself and offering to *go* to Los Angeles to buy them lunch if he could have ten minutes of their time. Six of these people wrote him back, and Kyle travels to LA twice a year to meet with them, ask questions, and learn the moviemaking craft.

Recently Kyle's efforts were rewarded at the Eclipse Awards for excellence in film, television, and online content from content creators in Michigan. Kyle and members of his team took home nearly every award for his film *The Acorn*. Kyle himself won Best Director for a Short Film, Best Screenplay for a Short Film, Best Editor in Narrative, and, along with Don Chase and Reid Petro, he won Best Short Film.[7]

That's not all. In addition to making films, Kyle is *going* in other ways nearly every day. Kyle runs. Weather permitting, he runs eight miles a day just for kicks. On one occasion, Kyle ran and told us, "Yeah, one day, I was out running, and I just sort of forgot to stop." I asked him, "How far did you go?" He responded, "Well, I went thirty miles." (What?? Kyle *accidently* ran over a marathon!! No words.)

I asked him why he ran every day. "One of the reasons I run nearly every day is because I want to develop the inner habit of not quitting." He runs so he doesn't quit. *#Genius!* This is *going* on steroids.

But wait, there's more. Kyle wanted to learn to play a particular musical piece on the piano. So, four to five times a week, he practices the piano as he teaches himself how to play the *Moonlight Sonata* (third movement) by Beethoven. (Obviously.)

I am inspired by Kyle's story and his daily habits to pour into the creative reinvention of multiple areas of his life. But my favorite part of Kyle's story is while he is succeeding at all of his extra endeavors, he is just as diligent at maintaining his commitment to the Lord and helping to build the church.

So. Be like Kyle!

What could you do every day?

Read one chapter in Proverbs.
Pray for the president when you wake up.
Text your parents and/or kids before bed.
Send ten emails to prospective customers.
Read a book.
Listen to a podcast.
Laugh at noon.
Buy someone a cup of coffee.
Write 1,000 words.
Smile at your coworkers.
Hold a plank for thirty seconds.
Dance to an upbeat song for three minutes.
Do twenty-five jumping jacks.
Thank the Lord.

The point is, you have to get the party started. You have to get in the race. You must get going. And the truth is, it won't be great at first. I love what my friend Alli Worthington posted in her Instagram feed (@alliworthington)—it's true!

Your first podcast will be awful.
Your first video will be awful.
Your first article will be awful.
Your first art will be awful.

Your first photo will be awful.
Your first game will be awful.
But you can't make your 50th without making your first.
So, get it over with and make it!

Your reinvention gets real when you answer Reinvent Question #3: What will you do? It's time to *go and get this party started*!

## reinvention review

1. In what ways does this chapter fire you up to *go, get this party started* and reinvent?
2. What is the biggest thing that hinders you from starting? How will you overcome it?
3. What one thing will you do today to get started on reinventing your life?

## chapter 20

# borrow, baby, borrow

*I don't think anybody steals anything; all of us borrow.*

B. B. King

He didn't invent shampoo. He *borrowed* it.

John Paul DeJoria turned shampoo into a multi-billion-dollar business when he cofounded the Paul Mitchell hair care system with stylist Paul Mitchell. The once homeless DeJoria had a strong work ethic and a positive attitude, and slowly but surely he made his black-and-white bottles of shampoo famous. Regarding his success, he says, "Don't expect it to be easy. Be prepared for a lot of rejection, because you are going to get it. If you are prepared for it, it's not going to hurt you as much... Be just as enthusiastic on door 101 if 100 have been closed in your face. Eventually you're going to do it."

As an adult, he worked a series of odd jobs, from janitor to door-to-door encyclopedia salesman. He was fired multiple times and was homeless twice, roaming vacant lots for soda pop bottles to cash in for spare change to buy food for his then-toddler son. Eventually, it all paid off. In addition to the incredible success he's had with building his hair care business,

he's been just as generous in giving money away and was Variety's 2017 Philanthropist of the Year.

In Austin, Texas, where he lives most of the year, DeJoria walks around homeless neighborhoods handing out $100 bills to "people who look like they're really down on their luck and need a break."[1]

What does DeJoria's story mean for us? Simple. When it comes to what you'll do, you don't have to worry about being original! You can and must borrow things that already exist.

The Maven understood this, and we can learn a lot from her story. Let's continue answering Reinvent Question #3.

## reinvent question #3: what will you do?

The Maven was told to "borrow" jars—a lot of jars. The good news is that she didn't have to originate, create, and innovate everything from scratch. She didn't have to throw clay on the potter's wheel to design her own original jars.

She was told to *borrow* existing jars. She could "borrow" from her friends and neighbors. Borrowing is interesting. It was probably humbling. It might have been embarrassing for her and her boys to run up and down the street collecting empty containers in their wheelbarrows.

Nonetheless, her job was to borrow jars from her neighbors—not just a few but to borrow big! Little did the Maven know that the degree to which she borrowed was the degree to which God performed His miracle in her life. The size of her reinvention miracle was going to be contingent on her faith and obedience—that is, on how many vessels she *borrowed*, not on how much oil God *supplied. #boomdeahdah*

In other words, God was willing to fill as many vessels as she had the faith to borrow!

### it's okay to borrow

Sometimes, we get stuck thinking everything we do has to be original or we have to do it all by ourselves. But there's no shame in borrowing and seeking help from others.

To reinvent your life spiritually, relationally, financially, and in every other way, let's talk about what you could borrow:

Borrow ideas.
Borrow technology.
Borrow from the past.
Borrow in collaboration with others.
You can borrow on existing products or services.
Borrow the hard work and resources others have made available.
Borrow by reading, observing, and exposing yourself to what others are doing.

Here are a few examples of the types of borrowing you should consider:

**Borrow the alphabet.** Are you trying to reinvent and revive your relationship with the Lord? Borrow the alphabet! Pam, a friend of mine, reinvented her worship life by praising the Lord using each letter of the alphabet in her daily time with the Lord—she thanks Him for being *Amazing, Beautiful, Conqueror Delightful,* and twenty-two other words that begin with the remaining letters of the alphabet to exalt Him.

**Borrow a pit crew.** Trying to reinvent a process at work?

Look what happened when a team of heart surgeons from the Great Ormond Street Hospital in London borrowed ideas from the Ferrari pit crew. They shaved microseconds off patient transfers from the operating table to the recovery room—a critical time for patients. After meeting with the Ferrari pit crew and borrowing from their processes, these heart surgeons reinvented their own processes and increased their patient transfer speed by 65 percent! They collaborated with experts and borrowed wisdom to make something better. The good news is after this collaborative effort, Ferrari became a sponsor of the hospital.[2]

**Borrow something old-school.** Why not revive the past? Remix old songs? Remake old movies? Reinvent the classics? What about bringing back drive-in movie theaters? Samsung is borrowing from the past—they're bringing back the "flip phone" by reinventing mobile phones with a new old-school concept.[3]

Ever thought of reinventing the wheel—on a 3D printer? HRE Wheels and GE Additive are! They just codeveloped the first 3D-printed titanium wheel.[4]

**Borrow from the circus.** Quebec-born Guy Laliberté didn't invent the circus; he borrowed it and reinvented it. He started out playing the accordion, eating fire, and walking on stilts as a street entertainer, but in 1984 it was time to get going to do something different! So he reinvented the circus when he cofounded Cirque du Soleil—a fresh, innovative concept for a circus without animals! (Up until that time, the circus had been defined by Ringling Bros. and Barnum & Bailey.)[5]

In 1987, Cirque du Soleil launched their first tour in the United States with their "We Reinvent the Circus" performance. Their unique, bold, colorful set designs, costumes, and creative performances wowed fans! Today, Cirque du Soleil shows have been seen by over 150 million people around the world, something that

took Barnum & Bailey's circus over one hundred years to achieve. With dozens of shows currently running around the world, they now employ over 5,000 people. Laliberté borrowed.[6]

**Borrow public domain.** Want to reinvent a classic? What about the thousands of works that are now part of "the public domain" and up for grabs? You can revive, remix, and reinvent old books, classic songs, and original plays. If you're a visionary with a creative gift, you can borrow from history and reinvent those works for these times. Just as Solomon said, "There is nothing new under the sun."

**Borrow coffee.** Think about the "borrow" effect when it comes to Starbucks! Howard Schultz didn't invent coffee; he borrowed a concept he saw in Italy. He perked up the ordinary! (Pun intended.)

Years ago, in a land far away, you could buy a cup of coffee for fifty cents at the gas station! Then suddenly, a new kind of coffee showed up when Schultz brought the Italian coffee bar to the United States. We went from paying fifty cents for a cup of coffee to waiting in line for a fancy $5 cup of joe. Hello, Starbucks. What did he do? He spotted an opportunity, borrowed an idea, put his spin on it—and reinvented a whole culture![7]

**Borrow the telephone.** How about Steve Jobs? He didn't invent the telephone. But he did borrow the ordinary, functional phone and reinvented it into a piece of art—not to mention one of the best-selling phones of all time!

**Borrow the surfboard.** Think about what's been done with the surfboard. Invented in 1926, to date there are more than thirty reinventions of the surfboard, including the skateboard, wakeboard, longboard, windsurf board, kiteboard, snow skis, snowboard, paddleboard, Snurfer board, snow skates, and other variations that have been "borrowed" from the original surfboard design.[8]

**Borrow air.** How about reinventing the classic car seat for little ones? Volvo has developed a new rear-facing car seat that inflates with air in forty seconds! According to Business Insider, "It only weighs 11 pounds, which is about half the weight of a regular car seat. Deflated, it fits neatly into a backpack, especially convenient for parents traveling with a child. The reinvented car seat, made with a fabric that can sustain high internal pressure, was originally developed by the military and is now used by the boating industry. There's no word on when the inflatable seat could come to market, but hopefully it will be soon."[9]

What can you borrow? What's ordinary in your world? What existing product or ideas could you borrow and improve upon?

**Borrow your niece.** What about social media? Anyone have it figured out? Let me share my tongue-in-cheek Instagram story with you because sometimes, when we aren't knocking it out of the park, we have to find the bright side and lighten up.

I bought Aimee Song's book *Capture Your Style* and was intrigued by her story of being an Instagram lifestyle blogger. She posts gorgeous photos of her travels, fashion, and lifestyle, and with over five million followers, she knows a thing or two about social media—so why not borrow her ideas?

I also bought the book for Tiffany, my niece (keyword: *millennial*), and we decided we were going to follow Aimee's advice and *borrow* all her tips, crack the code, and grow our social media followings. Well, my niece cracked the code and I just cracked. She grew her following to over 15,000 in the first year and I was stuck at 5,000. I must not have borrowed enough secrets—but my niece sure made the most of it!

I'm pretty sure there are more important things than social media, so let's move on and continue our conversation about reinventing *your* life!

(Oh, um, but before you go to the next chapter, would you

mind taking a really cool pic of you holding this book—and then would you post it, tag me, and hashtag the heck out of it? *Wink. Laughing Tears. Monkey Hand Over Mouth. Peace.*)

I hope you're enjoying this reinvention process! When it comes to answering Reinvent Question #3: What will you do?—*borrow, baby, borrow*!

## reinvention review

1. How does the idea of *borrow, baby, borrow* set you free and inspire you to reinvent?
2. When you think about borrowing, what ideas came to you as you read this chapter?
3. What hinders you from borrowing?

## chapter 21

# shut the door and pour

*Those who live to bless others*
*will have blessings heaped upon them,*
*and the one who pours out his life to pour out blessings*
*will be saturated with favor.*

Proverbs 11:25 TPT

Tim Tebow is a household name and a man of pure heart. No one can deny he has *poured* his heart and soul out on the football and baseball fields, in book writing, through his media endeavors as a sportscaster, as a TV host, and in moviemaking, and most notably, through his Night to Shine events, which give 75,000 special-needs teens a chance to attend their own prom.

In the natural, temporal things of life, he has poured out and achieved a good bit of success, while at the same time pouring out in the spiritual, eternal things of life and making an eternal difference in the lives he's touched. But Tim Tebow has had his share of disappointments and reinventions. In his book *Shaken*, he candidly talks about his journey:

> Being normal is safe. And easy. It doesn't require much work or effort or change on our part. But it always leads to mediocrity. When we strive to be just like everyone else, we never have a chance to be special. When you start to embrace and even celebrate how special and different God made you, you can begin to do extraordinary things. You can begin to see yourself through His eyes. You can begin to live in the uniqueness with which you were created. You can be motivated and inspired to go against the grain.[1]

What about you? What does it mean to pour out what you have? Let's talk about it as we continue answering Reinvent Question #3.

### reinvent question #3: what will you do?

The Maven had a little pot of anointing oil and a lot of borrowed empty jars. Now what?

Twice she was told to "shut the door and pour" out the oil she had. When she and her sons began to pour the oil into borrowed jars, God touched it! God multiplied her anointing oil and filled every empty jar they had!

When she and her sons looked around, they had a whole garage full of oil inventory! God's oil that is black gold, Israel's ~~Texas~~ tea! The next thing you know, the old Maven's a millionaire! (Couldn't resist. *#unclejedwouldbeproud*)

Through the process of obediently pouring out behind closed doors, she went from being a desperate single mom to becoming an oil tycoon!

In the same way that God touched and multiplied the Maven's oil, He wants to touch and multiply your life. And as it turns

out, the God-touch often happens when we are pouring out behind closed doors. Are you in a "shut the door and pour" season? What has the Lord told you to pour out?

In your case, it may not be oil you are pouring out. You may need to pour out time in developing your business plan, contacting buyers, or building your company.

It could look like pouring out in the wee hours to work on legislation, to serve in an emergency room, or to patrol your city and keep it safe.

It may be pouring out your heart on the keyboard to write a book, pouring out on the piano to write a song, or pouring out in conversation to comfort the lonely.

It could be pouring your time into the people who live in your house by being a stay-at-home mom, homeschooling your kids, or playing catch with your son.

It may mean pouring out at work in engineering a solution, leading product development, making sales calls, or pouring into your team, staff, or volunteers.

It might be a season of pouring out your heart in prayer, in seeking God and growing in His Word.

I don't know anyone who embodies this idea of "pouring out" more than Dodie Osteen (*Joel Osteen's mom*). In her eighties, she's filled with love and compassion for others. She still drives around her beloved city of Houston, praying for those who live there. Ever since the Lord healed her of incurable liver cancer nearly forty years ago, she's poured out in prayer for the sick—whether in person or long distance.

A few years ago, I reached out to Dodie (my adopted Texas mama) and asked for her prayers regarding a particular challenge I faced. She prayed for me and shared several God-touched words—those anointed words filled me with assurance

and faith. Like the Maven, God has touched Dodie's "pot of anointing oil" and as she has *poured out*, He's multiplied it to fill thousands of empty vessels.

What about you? What does pouring out look like in your life?

When you follow His prompts to pour out what you have, He will touch, anoint, and multiply it—and in the process reinvent your life.

God does a lot when we "shut the door and pour."

He wants your success in life to be holistic—spirit, soul, and body—where you are prospering and in health just as your soul prospers (3 John 2). Again, that means succeeding in your relationship with the Lord and others, in your mental and emotional health, in your vocational and ministry endeavors, and in your physical health and wellness!

Behind closed doors, as you pour out, the Lord works in you "to will and do of His good pleasure" (Philippians 2:13). Behind closed doors, He matures you to be more like Him.

But here's the rub.

Pouring out behind closed doors is hard. Sometimes boring. It's where we are invisible. It's where we crucify our flesh. It's where we learn how to live in a countercultural way.

What I mean is this:

The world says, "Promote yourself. Climb the ladder. Step on whoever is in the way." Jesus says, "Humble yourself and God will exalt you."

The culture says, "Get all you can. Keep all you get." Jesus says, "Freely you have received. Freely give."

Society says, "Make a name for yourself. Look out for number one." Jesus says, "If you want to be great, be the servant of all."

People say, "You do you. Be confident. Live your truth." The Bible says, "Be like Christ. Put no confidence in the flesh. Jesus is the truth."

God's ways are the "opposite" of the world's ways.

When we pour out behind closed doors, our efforts, sacrifice, and labors for the Lord are not in vain. God sees it all. And it is in the pouring out that He works miracles—in us and through us.

Everyone's story and calling are different, but let me share a bit more of my journey with the hope that the principles I learned will help accelerate your "pouring out behind closed doors" season—or at least help you understand what God might be doing in your life.

## when you feel hidden and invisible

I had big plans to be a dentist, play tennis three days a week, and give money to gospel causes.

Until Debbie came to visit.

Debbie was on staff with Campus Crusade for Christ and I was a junior in college and the assistant director of Henry Hall at Western Michigan University. The day she came to visit, she had a mission to share a little green booklet called *Have You Discovered God's Will for Your Life?* with me.

At first, I was annoyed. (Yes, I had discovered God's will, thank you very much. Well, okay, "my will," but same thing. Anyhow...) Nevertheless, I was polite as Debbie shared the booklet.

When she got to this Bible passage, time stopped for me:

> For "Everyone who calls on the name of the LORD will be saved."
>
> But how can they call on him to save them unless they believe in him? And how can they believe in him if

> they have never heard about him? And how can they hear about him unless someone tells them? And how will anyone go and tell them without being sent? That is why the Scriptures say, "How beautiful are the feet of messengers who bring good news!" (Romans 10:13–15 NLT)

*Wait? What?*

Debbie continued talking, but I can't tell you what she said, because my eyes were glued to the Bible passage and I replayed it in my heart:

*Who could be saved?* Everyone who calls on the Lord.

*How could people call on Him?* They couldn't, unless they believed.

*How could people believe?* They couldn't, unless they heard.

*How could they hear?* They couldn't, unless there was a preacher.

God needs preachers?

God needs preachers!

It was as if the heavens parted over my dorm room and I sensed God speaking to my heart: *"I interrupt your life to bring you this very important message. You are not going to be a dentist. You're going to be a preacher."* After all, if God needed preachers, how could I be a dentist? (I had no idea what this actually meant, and I didn't even know if girls could be preachers. I found out later a lot of people didn't think so! *Wink.*) But if God needed preachers so people could hear, so they could believe, so they could call on the Lord, and so they could be saved, put me in, Coach! Here I am; send me.

It turns out this was a life-changing reinvention moment for me.

Soon after this visit with Debbie, I was in my dorm room when I had what I would call a mini-vision. (I tell you this not to sound special, but because it happened to me and was such

a huge part of my life's reinvention, and whether or not you've experienced something similar, I hope it encourages you to remember what the Lord has shown you about your own life.)

In the first scene of this mini-vision, I saw myself standing on a platform in a large auditorium teaching the Bible. As clear as day, I could see it. I questioned within myself, *I'm going to speak?*

In the next scene of the mini-vision, I saw numerous bookshelves in what looked like a bookstore. I walked toward the bookshelves, and when I looked at the spine of those books, I saw my name. Again, I questioned, *I'm going to write books?* (This was as surreal as it sounds. I was a baby Christian. I wasn't a speaker or a writer. I was a biology major who wanted to be a dentist. The thought of speaking or writing a book had *never* crossed my mind.)

After this mini-vision, which lasted no more than a minute or two, I hid all of this in my heart. I didn't dare tell anyone until many, many years later.

Through those two experiences—the Romans 10 meeting with Debbie and the mini-vision—it seemed as if God threw the "go ye" bone (the "go ye into all the world and preach the gospel" bone...) and like a good little puppy, I was ready to quit school, run after that bone, and pour out my life to preach the gospel to the world—or so I thought.

Instead, I felt led to change my major from biology (guess I won't need that chemistry class!) to communications and transfer to Boston University to await further instructions.

Little did I know that the Lord was about to have me "shut the door and pour" behind the scenes for years, often feeling hidden, underutilized, overlooked, invisible, and unknown. His purpose was to help me learn, grow, and mature in various seasons of reinvention.

The reinvention process I experienced is not unique to me.

It's very possible you are in a season of reinvention where you feel stalled out: unseen, unnoticed, and unrecognized. God sees you and He's working a plan that will make more sense at some point.

Remember what Jesus said: "You do not realize now what I am doing, but later you will understand" (John 13:7 NIV). It's true—later you will understand.

During those behind-the-scenes years in my life, I did multiple things: finishing up at Boston University and then attending Rhema Bible Training College, getting married, then trying to be a good wife and raising toddlers, and eventually working on the administrative logistics to help my husband pioneer a church. In those seasons, I often wondered how, where, and when I would get to do the mini-vision stuff He showed me! I wanted to lead people to Christ, write bestselling books, and preach the Word to the masses—and I was, except for the *bestselling* and *masses* part.

What I didn't know is that often, when we want to run in hot pursuit of our dreams, goals, ambitions, and vision—when we are ready to fetch that "go ye" bone—the Master often says, "Stay!" (Turns out He's looking for people who will obey His voice.)

By "stay" He means for us to sit at His feet and pour out our pot of oil behind closed doors (where we're a nobody, anonymous, and undiscovered for a few ~~days~~ decades). All the while we're staying and pouring out, He's refining, sharpening, and polishing us. When we feel hidden, we aren't forgotten. I found this passage encouraging:

> Before I was born the LORD called me;
> from my mother's womb he has spoken my name.
> He made my mouth like a sharpened sword,

**in the shadow of his hand he hid me;**
**he made me into a polished arrow**
and concealed me in his quiver. (Isaiah 49:1–2 NIV)

I found out "staying" means *shut the door and pour* this way...

Pour into others.
Pour out in prayer.
Pour into growing in Christ.
Pour yourself into studying the Word.
Pour out in worship, faith, and loving God.
Pour into loving your husband, kids, and family.
Pour into cultivating new skill sets and experiences.
Pour into praying for and serving your friends and church.
Pour into being faithful at work and not easily offended.
Pour everything you have into helping someone else's ministry succeed.
Pour out every day with joy even if no one says thanks or gives you the credit.
Pour out the love even when you're hurt and feel betrayed by those you poured into.

Oh, and to *stay* and *pour* means "rejoice always," even when you're not yet doing the things you have in your heart, and when you feel used, stretched, unappreciated, criticized, and tired.

Yep, and while you're at it, "Do not let any unwholesome talk come out of your mouths, but only what is helpful for building others up according to their needs, that it may benefit those who listen. And do not grieve the Holy Spirit of God" (Ephesians 4:29–30 NIV).

Hello? Is this mic on? Are you still out there?

I found out this "shut the door and pour" part of the reinvention process can take years. It turns out, Joseph, Moses, David, John the Baptist, Paul, and Jesus Himself all experienced decades of prep time, where they were largely hidden, unrecognized, and unknown.

Jesus talked about it:

> Most assuredly, I say to you, **unless a grain of wheat falls into the ground and dies**, it remains alone; but if **it dies, it produces much grain**. He who loves his life will lose it, and he who hates his life in this world will keep it for eternal life. If anyone serves Me, let him follow Me; and where I am, there My servant will be also. If anyone serves Me, him My Father will honor. (John 12:24–26)

Let me share more of our story along with some color commentary. I have a sense that whether you're single or married, a stay-at-home parent, working for minimum wage, running your own business, or serving in full-time ministry, you'll be humored by our experiences and encouraged in your own!

## when god touches and multiplies

As a young married couple, with a little bit of life experience and several years of ministry training under our belt, Jeff and I were loaded with vision and we moved to Michigan to start a church.

It was a disaster! The church was so uninspiring that we didn't even want to attend it! After ten weeks of torture (I mean ministry), we canceled the so-called church and told the ten people attending to find a real church. We went back to faithfully

pouring out our hearts in prayer behind closed doors. Suffice it to say that during this "pouring out" season, we both *died to self*—and to our own grandiose ideas of ministry.

It was a very discouraging season and just like the Bible says, "Hope deferred makes the heart sick" (Proverbs 13:12). That was us.

After our dreams and ambitions had been dead for about eighteen months, the Lord resurrected the vision to plant a church in my husband's heart. (I was not amused! *Smile.*) When Jeff asked me what I thought about pioneering another church, my initial "faith-filled" response was, "Please no!!"

Needless to say, he felt he had heard from the Lord, so we planted Valley Family Church!

One fine September morning, we held our grand opening service in a rented lodge and when 120 people showed up, it felt like heaven touched earth! We were thrilled!

Week after week, it was easy to see God's hand of blessing upon this church plant. Turns out, hope deferred doesn't last forever; "when the desire comes, it is a tree of life" (Proverbs 13:12).

At last! We hit our stride and we enjoyed the season of growing the church, raising our four kids, and loving life. Just like the Maven's pot of oil, God was touching and multiplying our whole life and ministry. This reinvented fruit was tasty!

Then, when the church was about ten years old, the Lord reminded me of the mini-vision He had given me about writing books and speaking. By this time, I'd written a few books and done some speaking, but nothing like what I saw in that mini-vision. And that's when God said, "Fetch!"

## when god says, "fetch!"

My husband and I were at a pastors conference when the last speaker of the day, none other than Anne Graham Lotz (Billy Graham's daughter), got started on her message.

That's when I heard the Lord speak to my heart: "Fetch!"

Whaaat? Fetch? Now? Anne's message was not about "fetching"—but I knew this was a God-word about writing and speaking. A word I had previously waited and waited and waited to hear! I was taken by surprise, because to be honest, I had "stayed" and poured out for so long that by the time He said, "Fetch," I had almost forgotten about it. I wasn't the eager, energetic, or idealistic twenty-year-old I had been. But I had learned to listen to His voice.

So, "fetch" I did!

I have been "fetching" ever since!

God is faithful! When I look at His touch on our lives and the opportunities He has given us to minister around the world, the friendships we've made, the blessings He's poured out on our family, and the fruit we've seen through it all, it's definitely made all those years of faithfully "staying" and "pouring out behind closed doors" worth it.

Can you relate to parts of our story? Where are you in the process of "staying" and "pouring out behind closed doors"?

You may feel hidden, overlooked, and invisible, but the Lord sees you faithfully pouring out to serve His cause by loving others, serving your family, protecting your community, caring for your employees, building your business, and fulfilling your call. He sees your late nights and your early mornings, your tears and your joy, your weariness and your faithfulness.

He sees it all and He is working a plan!

As you answer Reinvent Question #3: What will you do?—

remember, God will touch and multiply things in your life when you *shut the door and pour*!

## reinvention review

1. In what ways does the idea of *shut the door and pour* inspire and challenge you?
2. Have you ever sensed the Lord asking you to "stay" when you really wanted to "fetch"? Describe it.
3. For you, what is the most challenging part of feeling hidden or invisible behind closed doors?

chapter 22

# ring the bell and sell

*More money will come your way this week if you* ~~(type AMEN and SHARE)~~ *worked last week.*

Social Media Meme

I'll never forget an airplane ride from Kalamazoo to Minneapolis. My husband and I had been praying for extra income. As church planters with four little kids, we needed creative ideas for extra funds. As we flew to a pastors conference in Minneapolis, "the knowledge of a witty invention" entered my heart! I've always been a baby boomer culture lover, and on our flight, the idea for a fun book started flowing. I pulled out a pen and several airline napkins and began writing 150 questions as fast as I could (this was many years before mobile phones and laptop computers). Who is Mrs. Beasley? What are the lyrics to the *Gilligan's Island* theme song? What is the name of Jonny Quest's dog? What are Red Ball Jets? What are the names of all the Brady Bunch members? and 145 other questions from my childhood.

It's a longer story, but when I returned home, I went to work establishing a small publishing company called Bell Bottom Books with exactly one book: *The Baby Boomer's Little Quiz Book—150 Questions to Prove You Really Grew Up Wearing Bell Bottoms.*

I finished writing the book, designed a cover, and off it went to a local book manufacturer. A few weeks later, we rented a delivery truck to pick up pallets of books from the printer and we stacked them in our garage. Now what?

Sell the books!

It was Good Friday and I called the head book buyer of a large chain of department stores in Michigan to see what he thought of the sample book I had sent him. I was so nervous making that call and surprised I got through to him—and even more surprised that he liked my book! (I literally had no idea how to sell anything, but sometimes acting like you know what you're doing is half the battle.) In any event, he said yes to carrying my book in all of his stores! (It was a *good* Friday!)

Within a few short months, this "witty idea" went from theory on napkins to reality on bookshelves. Several years into the process, another publisher picked up the book and Hallmark carried it in their stores. As a result, we were able to bring baby boomers a few enjoyable memories and we enjoyed the financial rewards of a witty idea! *#bellbottombooks*

The moral of the story? Next time you're on an airplane, listen for a witty idea!

> I, wisdom, dwell with prudence, and find out knowledge of **witty inventions**. (Proverbs 8:12 KJV)

The Lord has witty inventions for you to discover, create, and sell! Let's explore this as we continue to answer Reinvent Question #3.

## reinvent question #3: what will you do?

Let's review the progression of the Maven's reinvention.

First, she was told to "go" and she went!

Second, she was told to "borrow" and she borrowed.

Third, she was told to "pour" and she poured.

Fourth, she was told to "sell" and she sold.

God gave the Maven all the reinvention potential in the world with her big inventory of oil and then Elisha told her simply, "Go sell the oil." It was up to her to monetize it. In fact, to experience her reinvention and save her sons, it was *essential* that she sell the oil. (Right there, the first essential oils saleslady!) Oil was her niche.

Maybe you have a great idea or fantastic product, but you're not knocking it out of the park in sales? I've met many, many Christians over the years who felt the Lord had given them a brilliant idea, product, or service to reinvent their lives, but it never seemed to get off the ground. Why? Perhaps the ability to stay focused on selling was a struggle. The truth is, unless you are independently wealthy, you'll have to find a way to monetize your product, talent, expertise, or service. Even if you're in the nonprofit sector or leading a ministry, you'll have to "sell" (persuade) donors to give to your worthy cause.

That's why it's important to get serious about "selling the oil."

This is where reinvention gets fun! Call it sales, marketing, evangelism, communication, promotion, persuasion—whatever you prefer—you have to sell people on the value of what you have. Whether you're trying to make sales quotas to hit your bonus, persuade donors to help you with your ministry, or launch a new online business, you've got to "sell the oil!"

When God gives you an idea, a dream, a service, a product, a ministry, a company, an expertise, or a boatload of inventory,

your story isn't over—now you have to sell it. This is no time to over-spiritualize things. Done right, you exchange what you have for a fee (or donation) and everyone benefits. Selling is a win-win for both—the buyer and the seller.

In case you struggle with this idea of promotion, marketing, and sales, listen to what Jesus said: "Would anyone light a lamp and then put it under a basket or under a bed? Of course not! A lamp is placed on a stand, where its light will shine" (Mark 4:21 NLT). In other words, you wouldn't go to all the trouble to land a sales position, start a business, launch a church, create a product, or develop your expertise and then hide it! No, you put it in a prominent place where its light will shine.

No one will sell, promote, communicate, or persuade others to believe in or buy from you more than *you*. Remember, God doesn't sell the oil—you do. When you believe in your "oil" and know the value it will bring to people, you'll want to promote it!

## you're an entrepreneur with an advantage

Ever heard of the Issachar brothers? "The sons of Issachar who had understanding of the times, to know what Israel ought to do" (1 Chronicles 12:32). You can be like the sons of Issachar. You can understand the times you're in and know what you ought to do.

Twenty years ago, who imagined a drone delivering products to your front door? Sending your kids to school in a driverless car? Starting a business, selling goods, and making a fortune without ever housing a product or actually meeting a customer? Did you ever think you'd purchase your dog, your bed, or

your car from your phone and have it delivered to your house? How about seeing your doctor online? Working out from your home, live and in real time with a fitness class in NYC? Could you imagine the ability to have a group video chat with your family and friends in all parts of the world? Do you still wonder how Big Brother tracks your digital footprint and knows you're looking for keto-friendly food and a book on taming your two-year-old?

What once seemed straight out of a sci-fi has fast become our reality. And the good news for those paying attention and listening to the Spirit is that all of these innovations mean niche opportunities are waiting for you!

Seth Godin hit the nail on the head: "The economy just gave you leverage—the leverage to make a difference, the leverage to spread your ideas and the leverage to have impact. More people have more leverage (more chances and more power) to change the world than at any other time in history."[1]

Here's where you have an advantage. Jesus promised the Holy Spirit would guide you and "show you things to come" (John 16:13).

You can count on that. He is still in the revealing business and as you ask for His help, He will give you understanding of the times to know what "tides and trends" are emerging and what niche markets you ought to pursue to "sell your oil" and impact the world!

Let's glean from a few entrepreneurs who have learned the art of ringing the bell to sell.

**The *Shark Tank* star.** Daymond John of *Shark Tank* fame understood the art of sales and promotion and went from zero to $350 million in six years! In first grade he was a pint-sized entrepreneur selling customized pencils to fellow first graders. In

high school, he waited on tables at Red Lobster. In his twenties, he had a great desire to be successful, but he was struggling.

His single mother saw something entrepreneurial in him and bought him a sewing machine. Together, they sewed wool hats, beanies, and a few other things. The hats caught on and started selling. Daymond got his big break when hip hop music came out and his friend LL Cool Jay (a former neighbor) offered to wear one of Daymond's beanies. He wore it in a Gap clothing commercial, and from there everything took off.

Sales were soaring. Clothing was his niche. To capitalize on his corner of the market, his mother mortgaged their home and took $100,000 of equity to put into his company. To get another cash infusion, Daymond's mother took out an ad in the *New York Times* that said, "Million dollars in orders, need financing." Thirty-three people responded. Of the thirty-three, only three people actually had the ability to help them—and one person did! This person helped to put Daymond John on the map. These days, as a member of the *Shark Tank*, Daymond is returning that favor to many would-be entrepreneurs.[2]

**MyPillow man.** We know him as the optimistic "MyPillow man," but Mike Lindell wasn't always a happy salesman trying to give you your best night's sleep. In 2004 he was a crack addict, a few years later he was divorced and hit rock bottom, and then, voilà, by 2011 he'd become a self-made millionaire!

It's been a long journey, but the entrepreneurial spirit and God's power helped Mike to reinvent his life and he gives the credit to God. Although it took many years to come to fruition, in 2004 the idea for MyPillow, a pillow that would hold its shape, came to him in a dream. "I got up in the middle of the night—it was about two in the morning and I had 'My Pillow' written everywhere in the kitchen and all over the house."

Lindell dove in to the project, convinced the dream came

from God. Through a series of events he began to make and sell MyPillow and eventually things took off! The only problem? He was still addicted to crack! In 2009, he hit rock bottom and asked God for help: "God, I want to wake up in the morning and never have the desire (to do crack) again." He was convinced God had bigger plans for him and said, "I woke up the next day—and you've got to realize this is years of crack addiction—I go, wow, something's different." He said that was the beginning of his freedom and the desire for any form of cocaine "was just gone."

The rest is history. MyPillow has gone on to great success, selling over thirty million pillows, employing over 1,500 people, and taking in revenues of $300 million.

Mike Lindell knew what he wanted, used what he had, sold the pillows, and reinvented his life. He is living the dream, literally![3]

I love his story because it gives hope to all of us. If God could turn a crack addict into a multimillionaire as he focused on selling, what could the Lord do for you?

> The biggest risk is not taking any risk... In a world that is changing really quickly, the only strategy that is guaranteed to fail is not taking risks.
>
> —Mark Zuckerberg, Facebook founder

## name your niche

What are other ways to think about selling or promoting your company, product, service, or organization? Let's talk about how to "ring the bell and sell" by naming your niche.

Jeff and I used to drive by a restaurant with a big sign: Chinese

Food and Donuts. They were probably very good at both, but we never stopped in. We didn't need Chinese food and donuts at the same time. We would have been more apt to give them a try if they had focused on one or the other, but not both. By trying to reach two completely different markets, they had not found their niche.

In life, in business, in ministry, it's impossible to be all things to all people—but with God's help you can name your niche with laser-like focus and monetize your product or service.

What word comes to your mind when I say Lululemon? Chipotle? Zara? Netflix? Xbox? TJ Maxx? Chick-fil-A? Aldi? When people think of you, your product, business, or service, what *one word* do you want them to think of? Giving your product a focus will help you name your niche.

In our ministry, while we offer many programs and ministry to all kinds of people, we are focused on two words: Family. Basics.

We are *Valley Family Church* because when people in Southwest Michigan think about a church for their families, we want them to think of us. We are focused on kids and families.

We call our outreach ministry *The Basics With Beth* because when people think about where to learn the basics about God, faith, and the Bible, we want them to think about us!

What one word do you want people to associate with your product or service? What's your niche? Let's look at several examples to stir up your ideas.

## meet a need

What needs could you meet to serve others and "sell the oil"? Let's look at several people who are doing it.

**GoPro.** Nick Woodman wanted to record his surfing adventures, but there was just one problem. He *needed* a camera to take pictures while he was riding the waves. No problem. He reinvented it! To capture his surfing adventures, he wrapped a disposable, waterproof camera to his wrist and just like that, GoPro was born! Today, GoPro has sold $1 billion worth of cameras.[4]

**The Diaper Deck.** As the father of four little kids, my friend Tim and his wife, Renee, knew all too well the challenge of changing a diaper in public! At the time, the fold-down diaper deck as we know it didn't exist—but that's when the Lord gave him a witty invention. Tim sent me an email with his story:

> A place to change a child's diaper in the bathroom was non-existent. And the thought of changing our baby on the dirty bathroom floor was appalling. I found myself thinking about a solution for this problem all the time. And then one day, the idea came: *A commercial fold-down infant changing table that attaches to a commercial bathroom wall.* For three years I thought about this invention.
>
> One Sunday I was sitting in church when my pastor read Proverbs 8:12, "I, wisdom, dwell with prudence, and find out knowledge of witty inventions" (KJV).
>
> When I heard that verse, I almost jumped out of my skin! At that moment, I seriously heard God speak to me in my heart, saying, "No more thinking about it. Now is the time. Create this invention. Pray, and I'll lead you step-by-step." I know that sounds crazy to some people but that was my experience, and to me, it could not have been more real.
>
> After three years, we had our patent. And I began to sell what we called the "Diaper Deck" to restaurants.

It was happening slowly and that was probably a good thing, because I did not have a solution to mass manufacturing yet.

I diligently and aggressively reached out to two corporations in particular—McDonald's and Sears. At that time, McDonald's was opening two new restaurants in the city and agreed to put Diaper Decks in them and test them for a year. After a year of testing, they allowed us to sell them to the McDonald's franchises to order them for their stores. And soon after, Sears put them in every restroom around the country. At the same time, States around the country also began ordering them for public rest stops.

Today, they are everywhere. And now, there are a large number of companies making and distributing these changing tables around the world.

From the moment the Lord spoke to me about inventing this product, I could see them everywhere! Not for one second did the vision of that ever escape my heart, so to have seen it come to pass is very satisfying. I thank God for the opportunity He gave me, and how He helped me every step along the way!

I love Tim's story! One thing that stands out to me is the simplicity of a product just begging to be created and the ripple effect his invention had on the culture. A few years ago, no public restrooms had a changing table and now every one does. He stepped out in faith and took a risk and his God-given invention was a catalyst for a cultural shift. What cultural changes could the Lord make through you?

**The Perfect Card Box.** Many summers ago, my sister Kelly wasn't planning on it, but she became an entrepreneur! She had one daughter getting married and another daughter graduating

from high school within months of each other. For both of those events, she was looking for a gift card holder that was personal, elegant, and unique. She was also looking for a way to display the girls' beautiful engagement and senior pictures. Her creative mind got going and the next thing you know she's in the garage gluing this, drilling that, and inventing a unique card box that not only kept cards safe and tucked away, but also beautifully displayed personal photos. The card box was a big hit at both events and following those celebrations, her phone began to ring with requests to borrow her card holder. That's when she realized the Lord had given her a winning design and she launched the Perfect Card Box®. Kelly had to educate herself in all things entrepreneurial, including importing products; developing a website; and learning online sales processes, marketing, search engine optimization (SEO), and the like. She's been making brides happy for over thirteen years now by meeting a need and selling her card boxes online all over the country![5]

## spot an opportunity

What opportunities and trends could you leverage to serve others and "sell the oil"? These people are doing just that.

**Going green.** Through consistently reinventing his construction business and being ahead of the curve on several "green" trends, our friend Frank has watched his business, SIR Home Improvements, skyrocket! In 2008, when many companies were going out of business, Frank was looking for ways to increase his sales and the Holy Spirit gave him an innovative revelation to focus on green energy solutions for homeowners. He developed the SIR Home Cares program, dedicated to making homes energy efficient and bettering the local community and the

world at large. According to estimates from Consumers Energy, his program has prevented nearly 777 tons of carbon emissions from polluting the atmosphere.

This Spirit-led business idea definitely increased sales and helped his company grow from $2.9 million annually in 2008 to over $9 million today. And Frank gives the Lord the credit: "This is what God does when we listen and act."

But that's not the whole story; it's his *why* that keeps him selling and his *why* is people. Frank uses his wealth and success to help veterans through his Baths for the Brave initiative, as well as in his extensive work with the National Alliance on Mental Illness. In addition, he and his wife, Connie, are focused on making an eternal dent through their generosity to organizations that further the gospel.[6]

**Creativity meets technology.** I love how young people are using their creative and technical gifts to spot opportunities and sell their expertise. Whether it's through copy writing, photography, videography, or social media blogging, they are on it. They've revived leather, reclaimed wood, and retrofit old-school campers—and they're making money at it!

While in college, our son, Eric, and a friend of his monetized their video production skills. Rather than focusing on his original idea of shooting weddings, he found a niche in producing high-quality virtual videos for a large home builder. Eric hired his older sister, Meghan, for his on-camera talent, and they created custom videos for each of the builder's model homes.

My friend Kaylah—a sixth-grade teacher who adores her job and the "little humans" she teaches—also found she adores writing (more than hall passes and on whiteboards), so she taught herself the art of hand lettering and calligraphy. She started doodling words on just about any surface she could find, and

people loved receiving her handmade gifts, décor, and wedding paraphernalia. She launched a small business to share her love of lettering by giving people "their most important words, in their most important moments, on their most important days." Kaylah is loving her new little side hustle and has named her niche.

Andrew, one of our neighbors, just sent out fliers to offer his "aerial drone photography services" where he'll take stunning, high-quality footage of your home for just $100. As he put it, "Our services are a fraction of the cost of our competition. That's because I'm only fourteen and don't have a car payment yet." He found his niche! (Go Andrew!)

**Recycle it.** Why not recycle and reinvent waste? Rothy's shoes is. In their own words, "Rothy's began as an idea to turn recycled, single-use plastics into something both beautiful and useful. Three years in, we've taken over 30 million plastic bottles destined for landfills and repurposed them into timeless, durable flats."[7]

**Digital everything.** The digital age has changed everything—forever! If you have a digital device and Wi-Fi, the playing field is as level as it's been and for those who will reinvent themselves and "sell the oil," there are countless opportunities!

I wonder what witty ideas and selling secrets the Lord has in store for you?

> What turns me on about the digital age, what excited me personally, is that you have closed the gap between dreaming and doing. You see, it used to be that if you wanted to make a record of a song, you needed a studio and a producer. Now, you need a laptop.
>
> —Bono

When you answer Reinvent Question #3: What will you do?—you'll be inspired to take some calculated risks to *ring the bell and sell*!

Now, let's turn our attention to the final question—Reinvent Question #4.

## reinvention review

1. In what ways does the challenge to *ring the bell and sell* inspire you to reinvent your life?
2. Has the Lord given you a witty idea? If so, how are you acting upon it? What one next step should you take?
3. Have you named your niche? What one word do you want people to think of when they think of you, your product, idea, service, or expertise?

section 8

# reinvent question #4: *why will you do it?*

## chapter 23

# heaven is counting on you

*You didn't choose me. I chose you.*
*I appointed you to go and produce lasting fruit.*
Jesus

How did my younger sister Rhonda, the one who loved fashion, go-go boots, jewelry, makeup, and hair spray, end up on the mission field? Rhonda was glam and glitz on the outside, but I can assure you she was guts and grit on the inside.

So, why did she and my brother-in-law Tim move to Mexico City almost twenty-five years ago to pioneer a church and a Bible school? Why did they leave their respective countries of origin, their family, their friends, and the comforts of home to reinvent their lives and serve people in a nation they'd never been to?

Simple. Heaven was counting on them.

In their season of seeking the Lord, He spoke to their hearts: "Go to Mexico City to plant a church and out of that will come a Bible school." So, they took a trip to "spy out the land," received the confirmation they needed, and did just what the Lord asked of them.

On the day they arrived in Mexico City, they weren't welcomed with a piñata party or a bag of tacos; instead they were stopped

by police, told they violated the traffic circulation rules, and would have to pay a $500 fine. Rhonda looked the officer in the eye and told him in English, "We came here to serve God. The money we have is from Him and because you did not advise us as foreigners of the law when we entered the city gate, we are not going to pay you one dime!" (Guts and grit!) The officer looked her in the eye and then . . . let them go! (They later learned that the fine should have only been fifty pesos, not 500 dollars!)

After more than twenty years on the mission field, in addition to raising their three children, they've planted two churches and seven Bible schools, and they now oversee a network of twenty-five churches (twenty-two of which were started by members of their own church).

By God's grace, they've put a dent in eternity.

What about you? When it comes to reinventing your life, what's heaven counting on you to do and what's your motivation to do it?

In our remaining chapters, we're going to revisit the Maven and explore her motivation for reinventing her life—her why—as we answer Reinvent Question #4: Why will you do it?

I want to encourage and stir you up in these three truths:

Heaven Is Counting on You
Heaven Is Cheering for You
Heaven Wants You to Love Life

## reinvent question #4: why will you do it?

A certain woman of the wives of the sons of the prophets cried out to Elisha, saying, "Your servant my husband is

> dead, and you know that your servant feared the LORD. And the creditor is coming to take my two sons to be his slaves."
>
> So Elisha said to her, "What shall I do for you? Tell me, what do you have in the house?" And she said, "Your maidservant has nothing in the house but a jar of oil."
>
> Then he said, "Go, borrow vessels from everywhere, from all your neighbors—empty vessels; do not gather just a few. And when you have come in, you shall shut the door behind you and your sons; then pour it into all those vessels, and set aside the full ones."
>
> So she went from him and shut the door behind her and her sons, who brought the vessels to her; and she poured it out. Now it came to pass, when the vessels were full, that she said to her son, "Bring me another vessel."
>
> And he said to her, "There is not another vessel." So the oil ceased. Then she came and told the man of God. And he said, "Go, sell the oil and **pay your debt**; and you and your sons **live on the rest**." (2 Kings 4:1–7)

The answer to the fourth reinvention question, *Why will you do it?* is embedded in the Maven's story and comes from these two phrases: *pay your debt* and *live on the rest*.

In this chapter, let's talk about the idea of *paying our debt*.

Why did the Maven go through her reinvention process?

Her "why" for reinvention was to pay a *financial debt* and save her boys. *That was the whole premise of her story!* Her creditors were counting on it.

Why do we go through our own reinvention process?

Our why is the same but different. While the Lord also wants us to be good stewards and pay our financial debts, we have a more important debt to pay—a *gospel debt*. Our "why"

for reinvention is to pay a gospel debt and help those around us to be saved. *That is the whole premise of His story!* Heaven is counting on us.

### we have a gospel debt

The truth is, all this talk about reinvention without a strong *why* isn't much more than an inspirational pep talk. After all, why would you spend the time and energy to discern what you *want*, then assess what you *have*, expend energy on what you *do* in order to reinvent your life, unless there was a greater *why*—a greater purpose—attached to it? Why go through the effort? Why sacrifice your time, money, and energy to reinvent your life, improve your personal well-being, start a new business, expand your circle of friends, launch an innovative product, and pay all your debts, but still lack what gives your life meaning?

Although a general reinvention in areas of your life might bring a degree of satisfaction, if there is not a greater eternal "why" attached to it, ultimately you will likely feel unfulfilled and incomplete. Something purposeful will be missing. The rhetorical questions *Why am I here? What's my purpose? Does my life matter?* would go unanswered.

That's why we must answer the granddaddy, secret-sauce reinvent question of them all: *Why will you do it?*

Solomon, the wisest man who ever lived, understood this.

> **"Everything is meaningless," says the Teacher, "completely meaningless!"**
>
> What do people get for all their hard work under the sun? Generations come and generations go, but the earth never changes. The sun rises and the sun sets, then hurries

> around to rise again. The wind blows south, and then turns north. Around and around it goes, blowing in circles. Rivers run into the sea, but the sea is never full. Then the water returns again to the rivers and flows out again to the sea. Everything is wearisome beyond description. No matter how much we see, we are never satisfied. No matter how much we hear, we are not content.
>
> History merely repeats itself. It has all been done before. **Nothing under the sun is truly new.** (Ecclesiastes 1:2–9 NLT)

A tad depressing, isn't it? After declaring the vanity of it all, he went on to say something hopeful:

> He has made everything beautiful and appropriate in its time.
>
> **He also has planted eternity** in men's hearts and minds [**a divinely implanted sense of a purpose** working through the ages which **nothing under the sun but God alone can satisfy**]. (Ecclesiastes 3:11 AMPC)

Solomon basically said, unless your "divinely implanted sense of eternal purpose" is tapped, everything else in life amounts to nothing—meaningless. That's why your "why" is huge! Living life with an eternal sense of purpose gives all the temporal dimensions of your life meaning.

This is a game changing way to live.

When you choose to live from the eternal perspective, your life makes sense and you find satisfaction.

But here's where it gets tricky. Eternal things are unseen. Temporal things are seen. It's easy to live for the temporal things you can see and feel—wealth, materialism, status, human love, fame, or possessions. It takes faith to live for eternal things

you can't see—God, truth, divine love, the condition of people's souls, heaven, hell, and the gospel.

> Therefore we do not lose heart. Even though our outward man is perishing, yet the inward man is being renewed day by day. For our light affliction, which is but for a moment, is working for us a far more exceeding and eternal weight of glory, while we do not look at the things which are seen, but at the things which are not seen. **For the things which are seen are temporary, but the things which are not seen are eternal.** (2 Corinthians 4:16–18)

The apostle Paul understood the eternal perspective. He knew heaven was counting on him. He was obligated to pay a gospel debt. He'd been saved from his sin and come to know Jesus in such a personal way—he wanted this for everyone. Paul had a revelation of the "why" behind the "what" of preaching the gospel and said:

> I have an obligation to discharge and a duty to perform and a **debt to pay**. . . .
>
> For I am not ashamed of the Gospel (good news) of Christ, for it is God's power working unto salvation [for deliverance from eternal death] to everyone who believes. (Romans 1:14,16 AMPC)

While Paul had an obligation to pay a gospel debt, so do we. Perhaps you remember this line from an old worship chorus: "He paid a debt He did not owe. I owe a debt I could not pay. Christ Jesus paid a debt that I could never pay." It's true: We can't pay for our own debt of sin—on the cross Jesus did that for us—but as an act of gratitude, we can pay our gospel

debt by loving and sharing Christ with everyone in our world. "Don't owe anything to anyone, except **your outstanding debt to continually love one another**" (Romans 13:8 TPT).

### how much do you have to hate somebody?

I know it sounds like a strange question, but it will make sense.

One of the most thought-provoking gospel debt comments I've ever heard came from the lips of avowed atheist Penn Jillette, of the Penn & Teller duo.

> I've always said that I don't respect people who don't proselytize. I don't respect that at all. If you believe that there's a heaven and a hell, and people could be going to hell or not getting eternal life, and you think that it's not really worth telling them this because it would make it socially awkward—and atheists who think people shouldn't proselytize and who say "just leave me alone and keep your religion to yourself"—**how much do you have to hate somebody to not proselytize? How much do you have to hate somebody to believe everlasting life is possible and not tell them that?** I mean, if I believed, beyond the shadow of a doubt, that a truck was coming at you, and you didn't believe that truck was bearing down on you, there is a certain point where I tackle you. And this is more important than that.[1]

Whoa. How is it an atheist understands the incongruence of a Christian who doesn't share Christ (proselytize) more than many Christians?

To share Christ, we must love God and we must love people.

People don't like being "preached at and judged," but they do like being "communicated with and loved." What does it look like in this context?

Love is empathetic. Love puts itself in the shoes of another. Feels what they feel. Love does not belittle. Love helps. As followers of Christ, we should mimic Him in these things. He loved the unlovable. Healed the sick. Cared for the widows. Loved the children. Spoke the truth to the smug.

Jesus noticed people. Don't we all appreciate those who notice us? Make us feel like we matter? Feel our pain when we're going through a loss or having difficulty or a down day? Sometimes, a smile, a hug, and an "I understand" is really all we want. As followers of Christ, we are supposed to be known for our love.

Love also tells the truth.

This is where it gets complicated.

At the same time we're being empathetic to the plight and suffering of another, love won't allow us to leave them lost. Love compels us to help.

And the truth is, we can help because Jesus is the answer to every question. Jesus will forgive, help, heal, free, and comfort people—that's the good news of the gospel. But how do we share the gospel in a way that is easily received? Sharing the truth about Jesus, sin, eternity, heaven, and hell is not always well received. It doesn't always make you the most popular person at the party. It's not easy to tell people a truth they may not want to hear. But if you think about it from a practical angle, how can we keep the truth to ourselves?

For example, if you were in Chicago and told me you wanted to go to New York City, I would tell you to head east on the highway and follow the signs to NYC. If I noticed you hopped on the wrong highway and were heading west toward Los

Angeles, my love for you would motivate me to text you and say, "Hey, stop! You're on the wrong highway. Turn around. To get to NYC, head east." Hopefully, you would appreciate the call, turn around (reinvent!), and get to your desired destination.

Wouldn't it be weird, and actually rude and unloving, if I saw you heading to LA and I didn't call you to let you know? (If I kept that information from you because I didn't want to offend you or I didn't want you to "unfriend" me, wouldn't that be selfish on my part and not very loving toward you?)

In the same way, when our family and friends tell us they want God's blessings and a home in heaven, we point them to Jesus, right? If they hop on a highway that is going the opposite direction from Jesus, because of our love for them, why wouldn't we let them know? As Jillette said, how much do we have to hate somebody to not tell them? Sometimes this is well-received and sometimes not. Sometimes people turn around and get to Jesus. Other times, you're criticized as being narrow-minded. Judgmental. Intolerant. Jesus called that persecution for His Name's sake (John 15:20). It comes with the territory.

Let me tell you my story of sharing the gospel with my family to encourage you. You may feel a burden for the eternal condition of your family or friends. I did. As the first person to become a born-again Christian in my family, and because my conversion to Christ was so dramatic, nothing consumed my prayer life more than praying for my family to come to know Jesus. I loved them to pieces and I didn't want to go to heaven without them! I was new in my Christian faith, not too polished at sharing Christ or paying my "gospel debt"; nevertheless, the Lord helped me—and I know that what the Lord did for our family, He will do for you and yours.

### you mean to tell me?

One summer, I was participating in a summer project of beach evangelism with Campus Crusade in Hampton Beach, New Hampshire. My mom and my three younger sisters drove out from Michigan to "rescue" me (they didn't understand my zeal for Christ and thought I was in a cult). While my mom and sisters were coming to "rescue" me, my friends and I were praying for an opportunity to share the gospel and for the Lord to "rescue" them.

After they arrived, we took a road trip and wouldn't you know, the conversation got to the topic of Jesus, heaven, and knowing God. In the process of our conversation, I shared John 14:6 with my mom:

> "Mom, Jesus said, 'I am the way, the truth, and the life. No one can come to the Father except through Me.'"
>
> My mother said, "*You* mean to tell me if I don't receive Jesus Christ as my personal Lord and Savior, I could spend eternity in hell?"
>
> I thought, *Whoa, I didn't exactly say that, but Lord you're helping her understand the bottom-line importance of this.*
>
> I responded, "Mom, I didn't say it—Jesus said, 'I am the way, the truth, and the life. No one can come to the Father except through Me.'"
>
> Again, she said, "You *mean* to tell me if I don't receive Jesus Christ as my personal Lord and Savior, I could spend eternity in hell?"
>
> I responded again, "Mom, I didn't say it—Jesus said it. He said, 'I am the way, the truth, and the life. No one can come to the Father except through Me.'"
>
> The third time, she said, "You mean to *tell me* if I don't

> receive Jesus Christ as my personal Lord and Savior, I could spend eternity in hell?"
>
> I responded, "Yes, Mom, that's what Jesus said."
>
> What she said next shocked me.
>
> She asked, "If you believe that is true, why did it take you a year and a half to tell your family?"

I didn't see that coming. Boy, did that get to me. I thought she might ask some of the usual questions I'd heard, like "How could a loving God send anyone to hell?" or "What about those who haven't heard?" (I knew how to answer those questions.) I wasn't expecting her response, but I was glad to know she got it! The truth is, I'd been trying to "be a light" to share the gospel with my family, but apparently not very effectively.

I learned that not only do people need to *see* us as believers "being a light" for Christ, but also it is essential they *hear* the gospel message. It's the foolishness of preaching that leads people to Christ. That's what Romans tells us, remember?

> For "Everyone who calls on the name of the LORD will be saved."
>
> But how can they call on him to save them unless they believe in him? **And how can they believe in him if they have never heard about him? And how can they hear about him unless someone tells them?** (Romans 10:13–14 NLT)

As believers, we have the privilege and responsibility of telling people the good news of Jesus.

Shortly after this "rescue trip," my mom and eventually all of my sisters gave their hearts to Jesus!

Then, within a two-year time period, the rest of my family—my dad and stepmom and my stepdad—all came to Christ! The Lord went to work in the hearts of my entire family and in total, seven people in my immediate family came into a relationship with Jesus. Jesus truly reinvented our family!

On top of that, I never expected God would call nearly sixteen of my family members (sisters, kids, in-laws, nieces, and nephews) into full-time ministry to pioneer churches and plant Bible schools in America, Mexico, and Brazil, but within a few decades, He did just that. I praise the Lord for all of this—nothing makes me happier! (If you're a first-generation Christian, you never know the reinvention ripple effect your witness for Christ will have on your family and generations to come. So, be bold.)

These days, my mom, dad, and stepdad have since gone to heaven and I can't think of anything that compares to the joy I feel in knowing they are there and being able to play a small part in leading them to the Lord.

When you think about Reinvent Question #4 and the *why* behind your desire to reinvent your life, there's nothing more satisfying and sobering than to pay a gospel debt knowing *heaven is counting on you*!

The writer of Proverbs summarizes this nicely:

> A life lived loving God bears lasting fruit,
> for the one who is truly wise wins souls. (Proverbs 11:30 TPT)

## reinvention review

1. In what way does the idea that *heaven is counting on you* challenge you to reinvent?
2. When you think about *paying your gospel debt*, how does the question "How much do you have to hate somebody?" impact you?
3. If you've never done this, make a list of everyone in your family and start praying specifically for them to hear the gospel, to call on the Lord and to be saved. Are you willing to share the gospel with them?

# chapter 24

# heaven is cheering you on

*Only one life, 'twill soon be past, only what's done for Christ will last.*

C. T. Studd

I did an unscientific survey one night when hanging out with a few friends, and I simply asked, "If you could reinvent your life, in what areas would you want to do so?"

It didn't take long to get their answers.

My Realtor friend said: "I want my life to matter for the Lord. I have more time now and want to serve the Lord."

My doctor friend said: "I think you think about 'reinventing' throughout your whole life—always asking, 'Am I making a difference?'"

My business owner friend said: "Leading people to the Lord is number one."

The closer we get to the second half (or end) of our lives, the more important this becomes—or as one person in their later years told me, "I want to do more for the Lord. I need to make up for lost time." The best news is you can!

Let's find out how as we continue answering Reinvent Question #4.

### reinvent question #4: why will you do it?

Why will you reinvent? To pay your debt! That was the Maven's motivation and it's ours, too!

The Maven owed a financial debt—that was the *temporal* point of her story—but we owe a gospel debt and that is the *eternal* point of our story.

Staying focused on eternity, sharing the gospel with those who have not yet received Christ, making disciples, and building His church are our ways of paying a gospel debt. Heaven gets excited about this!

I'd be lying if I told you that reinventing your life to pay your gospel debt is easy. It's extremely fulfilling—but it's not easy. Reinventing your life to produce eternal fruit is no joke. (Remember the fruitless tree we don't want to be, from way back at the beginning of the book?) To produce eternal fruit requires a strong "why," not to mention endurance, persistence, and faith! When you're leading, serving, teaching, influencing, and discipling others, you may want to give up multiple times in the same day. It often requires sacrifice, extra hours, little recognition, a pay cut (or straight up volunteer hours), loads of humility, more grace and faith than you think you have, a servant's heart, and a consistent, eternal perspective. It ain't easy or for the faint of heart! But you've got the goods and there's nothing more rewarding! Plus, heaven is cheering you on!

> Therefore, since we are surrounded by so great a cloud of witnesses [who by faith have testified to the truth of God's absolute faithfulness], stripping off every unnecessary weight and the sin which so easily and cleverly entangles us, let us run with endurance and active persistence the race that is set before us. (Hebrews 12:1 AMP)

## your eternal dent

Your role in paying a gospel debt has eternal ramifications and is more important than you may realize. You don't have to be a preacher or missionary to do it; God wants to use the gifts He's given you to reach people and impact eternity. Isn't that the wildest thing to think about? You can put a dent in eternity!

The truth is, we only have a few short years to invest our temporary lives on earth into something eternal. If you think of your life as a *temporary dot* on an *eternal line*, you can live exclusively for the *pleasure of your dot*, which is here today and gone tomorrow, or you can *invest your dot* into paying a gospel debt and truly *dent the eternal line*. (Did you follow that?) In other words, you can make an eternal difference with your life! Let me tell you about several friends of mine who are using their gifts and influence to reach people and impact eternity.

**In the gym.** Todd, a good friend and leader in our church, is a Realtor and developer and always has his sights set on reaching others for Christ and impacting eternity. For years, he's invited guys from all walks of life to do weight-training workouts with him early in the morning in his home gym, and they always finish up with a Bible reading. He calls it "the Soldier Academy." Todd also has another group of guys that come over to train with him in jujitsu. He cranks up the Christian music and afterward he likes to have "how's life" chats to encourage them in their faith. For Todd, it's all about training to fulfill the call to make disciples who follow Jesus.

**On the mission field.** Two friends of ours, Walker and Haley, felt God's call to the mission field and moved their family thousands of miles to serve the beautiful people in Africa. In a recent exchange we had on social media, he posted this: "I doubt I would be a career missionary if I didn't believe in hell." In other

words, he has a big *why*. Why would he and his wife and their kids leave their family, friends, and comforts of home to serve the Lord and others in a foreign land? Because he believes there is an eternal heaven to gain and an eternal hell to shun. He loves the Lord and he loves those God has called him to pastor. Love has obligated him to share the love of Jesus with those he's called to serve. Walker said, "Only heaven carries the true rewards and fruit of our life here. If there is no heaven and hell, then a lifetime sacrifice seems huge. But when you think of people spending forever apart from God, it really is a small price."

**On the streets.** After their careers in the Coast Guard, in addition to preaching the gospel and empowering pastors around the world, my friends Bruce and his wife, Elaine, decided to focus on "paying their gospel debt" by pouring into kids (orphaned by the AIDS epidemic) living on the streets in Uganda. Since 2013, they've been loving, teaching, and training these kids to be smart, mighty warriors for Jesus while helping them relocate back into families.

When your "why" is big enough, you can do anything. With an eternal perspective of the *unseen*, it's easy to pay your gospel debt in this temporary life of the *seen*. The psalmist understood this.

**Our days soon become years until our lifetime comes to an end,**
**finished with nothing but a sigh.**
You've limited our life span to a mere seventy years,
yet some you give grace to live still longer.
But even the best of years are marred by tears and toils,
and in the end with nothing more than a gravestone in a graveyard!
We're gone so quickly, so swiftly;

we pass away and simply disappear.
Lord, who fully knows the power of your passion
and the intensity of your emotions?
**Help us to remember that our days are numbered,**
**and help us to interpret our lives correctly.** (Psalm 90:9–12 TPT)

Help us "to interpret our lives correctly"! Yes, Lord, help us to maximize our lives for Your cause. How could you use your gifts to reinvent your life and priorities and impact others for eternity?

Whether you're sharing the gospel message with friends, serving your family to represent Christ, helping your pastor build your church, making disciples in His name, praying for your city, or helping the poor—*you* are paying a *gospel debt* and putting a dent in eternity. When you reinvent your life in this way, heaven celebrates and cheers you on! It doesn't matter if you're preaching to thousands in stadiums, serving in foreign lands, or giving a cup of cold water to the least of His followers, Jesus takes note.

And if you give even a cup of cold water to one of the least of my followers, you will surely be rewarded. (Matthew 10:42 NLT)

Let me tell you about my friend Shannon. She embodies this in her everyday life.

Shannon's been a part of our church for over twenty years. After going through a divorce she did not desire, she had to reinvent. And she did. She embraced her new season with loads of grace and love.

Shannon is a stunner, an amazing mom, and one of the most

servant-hearted people I know. At church, if we need a small-group leader, Shannon volunteers. If we need help with the high school students, Shannon volunteers. If we need someone to facilitate our Bible Basics class, Shannon volunteers. In fact, while facilitating a Basics class for us, she met Eric and they were married. (Heyyyy, all you singles—get yo-self in a Bible class!)

Oh, did I mention, she also works a full-time job and she always remembers to drop off a huge pan of macaroni and cheese to help feed the masses at someone's special event? Together, she and her husband, Eric, have four children, plus the kids they "adopt" from time to time. On top of that, Shannon founded a chapter of Kindness Acts 20.35, an outreach to help the homeless in Southwest Michigan.

Why does Shannon do all of this? She's decided to invest her temporary life into eternal things. She embodies the gospel command to serve others and she has given her life, time, and financial resources to pay a gospel debt. She hasn't just done this for a few months or even a few years...she's been doing this for decades!

The thing I love most about Shannon's reinvention is the balance she's found in taking care of herself, while at the same time serving her family, assisting the less fortunate, and helping to build the church!

Speaking of church...

## heaven's most important thing on earth

Building the church is the most important thing Jesus is doing on planet earth—everything else is peripheral. That's a big statement—and exactly what the Bible tells us.

I love how this is conveyed in the Message Bible:

> God raised him from death and set him on a throne in deep heaven, in charge of running the universe, everything from galaxies to governments, no name and no power exempt from his rule. And not just for the time being, but forever. He is in charge of it all, has the final word on everything. **At the center of all this, Christ rules the church. The church, you see, is not peripheral to the world; the world is peripheral to the church.** The church is Christ's body, in which he speaks and acts, by which he fills everything with his presence. (Ephesians 1:20–23 MSG)

Big things are happening in His church around the world. Make no mistake, Jesus is building His church! He's the Head and we are the Body, and that means our individual, God-touched reinvention will include a commitment to the thing He gave His life for—the church!

While there are still so many people to reach, every church leader we know is seeking the Lord on the reinvention game plan they need for attracting, connecting, evangelizing, and discipling people—with the timeless gospel message.

I can think of a few reinventions our church has gone through, and each one propelled it forward. A number of years ago, we were going through a generational and technological shift and updating everything. Our music, attire, stage, video, lighting, graphics, aesthetics, and our style of ministry. While the gospel message didn't change, everything else did. The problem is, we didn't cast enough vision to prepare the church for the changes. So, when we painted the sanctuary, turned down the lights, turned up the volume, and turned on the hazer, you can imagine the response! We instantly lost one hundred people—good people, stalwart believers. (Uh, Houston, we have a problem.)

Nonetheless, we sensed we were on target with what the

Lord wanted us to do, so we held our course and tried to do a better job casting the vision. By God's grace, within the next eight months, our church grew by 800 more people, and for two years in a row, our church was among the 100 Fastest Growing Churches in America as annually published by *Outreach Magazine*. The reinvention strategy was a winner, and we learned a few lessons on how to better lead change. (Let me give a shout-out here because in church life, it's normal for people to come and go for all kinds of reasons. But the longer we pastor, the more thankful we are for the incredible people who have been *with* us on the journey through many reinventions over the years. We don't know of a more genuine group of believers more passionate for the cause of Christ than our beloved VFCers. And, of course, we are biased! That is all. Carry on.)

A few years later, as we built and moved into a new facility, our church went through a transition in worship, and we were without a leader.

Our son Luke, all of eighteen years of age at the time, made a big reinvention decision. We didn't ask him to do this, but he felt the Lord leading him to move from the university he was attending (about ninety miles away) to come home, attend the university in our town, and lead worship for us. That was a massive help to us and our church. Our worship went to a new, fresh level—and we loved having him home!

What most people didn't know is that Luke was so nervous, he was in our office restroom throwing up before he had to lead worship! All the way to the sanctuary, we were cheering him on and reassuring him! His "why" for coming home to help us was his love for the Lord, the church, and his heart to invest in something eternal.

Years later, I love how God has rewarded and blessed his life—now married, he and his wife, Kelsey, attended Hillsong

College in Sydney, Australia, and have served on staff there while getting a taste of revival in one of the fastest-growing churches anywhere in the world.

Reinventing church is not for the faint of heart.

When you think about it, it's no small thing for any church funded by donations and staffed by volunteers to impact a community and change lives for eternity by reaching multiple generations of people, all with diverse opinions and preferences and who only attend an average of eleven to thirty-three weekends a year! (Standing O for all you pastors and church leaders!) The fact that church happens *at all* is a miracle freak of nature and proof that Jesus *is*, in fact, building His church!

What about you? What about your church? Can I challenge you to reinvent your priorities and schedule to help build your local church in a greater way?

### run to win

Paying a gospel debt is not a one-time event. And you may not see many rewards in this life. But one day, all of your prayers, obedience, generosity, sacrifice, and service to pay your gospel debt so others can come to Christ will be rewarded and celebrated. Keep running to win!

> Don't you realize that in a race everyone runs, but only one person gets the prize? So run to win! All athletes are disciplined in their training. They do it to win a prize that will fade away, but we do it for an **eternal prize**. (1 Corinthians 9:24–25 NLT)

This story is told of a missionary and his wife:

A missionary and his wife had been serving the Lord in Africa for many, many years. Having served on the mission field most of their lives, they were returning home—feeling a bit discouraged and their health deteriorating. On board the vessel, they realized they were on the same ship as President Teddy Roosevelt, who was returning from one of his big game hunting experiences. While sailing home, no one paid much attention to them, but they watched the fanfare that accompanied the President's entourage and passengers trying to catch a glimpse of the great man.

As the ship moved across the ocean, the old missionary said to his wife, "Something's wrong. Why should we have given our lives in faithful service to God in Africa all these many years and have no one care a thing about us? Here this man comes back from a hunting trip and everybody makes much over him, but nobody gives two hoots about us."

His wife said, "Dear, you shouldn't feel that way."

He said, "I can't help it. It just doesn't seem right."

When the ship docked in New York City, a crowd had gathered and the band was playing fanfare music to greet the president. The mayor and other dignitaries were there to welcome the president home. The newspaper was full of photos and news of the president's arrival, but no one noticed the missionary and his wife's arrival. They slipped off the ship, found a cheap apartment on the east side of town and hoped to find work to make a living in the city.

That night, the man's spirit broke. He said to his wife, "I can't take this. God is not treating us fairly."

> His wife replied, "Why don't you go into the bedroom and tell the Lord about it?"
>
> A short time later, he came out from the bedroom, but now his face was completely different. His wife said, "Dear, what happened?"
>
> "The Lord settled it with me," the man said. "I told him how bitter I was that the President should receive this tremendous homecoming when no one met us when we returned home. After I finished, it seemed as though the Lord put his hand on my shoulder and simply said, 'But you're not home yet.'"[1]

You are not home yet, either.

The Bible is loaded with promises of the eternal prize and rewards ceremony being prepared for those who have been faithful to the Lord (1 Corinthians 3:14; Revelation 22:12). And I won't even mention what the Lord has planned for you during the millennial reign of Christ on earth for 1,000 years . . . another time, another book, another reinvention.

Suffice it to say, God won't forget your labors of love!

When you think about Reinvent Question #4 and the *why* behind all of the reinvention work you are doing, there's nothing like spreading the gospel, making an eternal difference, and knowing that *heaven is cheering you on*!

All the people you invest in for the gospel's sake, these people ARE your reward! One day, you're going to be in heaven and you're going to look around and see others who are there because you faithfully followed the Lord and *paid your gospel debt*. You'll thank God He helped you reinvent your life to weather the storms and walk through the valleys. You're going to be glad you didn't quit. You'll be so glad you "paid your gospel debt" and it will all be worth it!

After all, what gives us hope and joy, and what will be our proud reward and crown as we stand before our Lord Jesus when he returns? **It is you!** (1 Thessalonians 2:19 NLT)

## reinvention review

1. How does knowing *heaven is cheering you on* encourage you in your reinvention?
2. When you think about paying your gospel debt by living your temporal life to impact eternity, how does that affect your priorities?
3. In what ways could you use your time and talents to help *your* local church?

## chapter 25

# heaven wants you to love life

*The joy of the Lord is your strength.*

Nehemiah

The Lord never intended for your life—or reinvention—to be dull, boring, or lackluster, so let's end our time together with a little gladness!

A little girl was talking to her teacher about whales.

The teacher said it was physically impossible for a whale to swallow a human because even though it was a very large mammal its throat was very small.

The little girl stated that Jonah was swallowed by a whale.

Irritated, the teacher reiterated that a whale could not swallow a human; it was physically impossible.

The little girl said, "When I get to heaven I will ask Jonah."

The teacher asked, "What if Jonah went to hell?"

The little girl replied, "Then you ask him."[1]

*#cymbalcrash*

How about another?

A woman arrived at the Gates of heaven.

While she was waiting for Saint Peter to greet her, she peeked through the gates.

She saw a beautiful banquet table. Sitting all around were her parents and all the other people she had loved and who had died before her. They saw her and began calling greetings to her: "Hello—How are you! We've been waiting for you! Good to see you."

When Saint Peter came by, the woman said to him, "This is such a wonderful place! How do I get in?"

"You have to spell a word," Saint Peter told her.

"Which word?" the woman asked.

"Love."

The woman correctly spelled "L-O-V-E" and Saint Peter welcomed her into heaven.

About a year later, Saint Peter came to the woman and asked her to watch the Gates of heaven for him that day.

While the woman was guarding the Gates of heaven, her husband arrived.

"I'm surprised to see you," the woman said. "How have you been?"

"Oh, I've been doing pretty well since you died," her husband told her. "I married the beautiful young nurse who took care of you while you were ill. And then I won the multi-state lottery.

"I sold the little house you and I lived in and bought a huge mansion. And my wife and I traveled all around the world. We were on vacation in Cancun and I went water skiing today. I fell and hit my head, and here I am. What a bummer! How do I get in?"

"You have to spell a word," the woman told him.

"Which word?" her husband asked.

"Czechoslovakia."[2]
*#shegotjokes*

I'm glad we are wrapping up the book with happiness, joy, and laughter because the reinvention of your life would not be complete without it. Just as C. S. Lewis said, "Joy is the serious business of heaven."

After all the effort you've put into processing your reasons to reinvent and answering the questions—what you want, what you have, what you will do, and why will you do it—we have to finish the book with joy!

With that in mind, let's revisit Reinvent Question #4 and the Maven one final time.

## reinvent question #4: why will you do it?

The last few words the man of God told the Maven are very important and tell us why:

> And he said, "Go, sell the oil and pay your debt; and you and your sons **live on the rest**." (2 Kings 4:7)

His last words to her (and to us) were "live on the rest." It would be easy to overlook these words, but we shouldn't.

Several meanings of the word *live* include "to have life, to live (prosperously), to revive from sickness, discouragement, faintness, death, to quicken, revive, refresh, restore to health, restore to life" and more![3]

In other words, "Single mom of two, once you sell the oil and pay your debt, you and your boys can *live* on the rest of the proceeds! It's time to put away your grief, be revived, encouraged,

refreshed, and restored to health, prosperity, and life! Hey, soul sister, it's time for you and your boys to love life!"

*It's a new day, Ms. Maven—Mission Reinvented: Accomplished!*

Sure, she had been through a lot of heartache. But just as the Scriptures say, there is a time for everything. "A time to cry and a time to laugh. A time to grieve and a time to dance" (Ecclesiastes 3:11 NLT). It's true for you, too. Though weeping may endure for the night, joy comes in the morning.

Why reinvent? Because God wants you to live—and to love your life!

It's time to quit crying *big salties* and start living life!

*Yep. Bye-bye, Kleenex.*

One of the best weapons we have is the ability to laugh, dance, and enjoy life! The truth is, if we don't choose joy and start laughing, we'll struggle with discouragement, sickness, and depression: "A joyful, cheerful heart brings healing to both body and soul. But the one whose heart is crushed struggles with sickness and depression" (Proverbs 17:22 TPT).

When you think about it, if heaven is going to be a place of eternal bliss, with joy unspeakable and full of glory, wouldn't it be just like the Lord to desire that His redeemed kids love life and experience some of that bliss now?

Perhaps that's why Jesus could say:

> I have told you these things, so that in Me you may have [perfect] peace and confidence. In the world you have tribulation and trials and distress and frustration; but **be of good cheer** [take courage; be confident, certain, undaunted]! For I have overcome the world. [I have deprived it of power to harm you and have conquered it for you.] (John 16:33 AMPC)

## god wants you to enjoy life

Did you know, God has nothing against you enjoying your life? In fact, He encourages it. Jesus told us it's one of the reasons He came. "But I have come to give you everything in abundance, more than you expect—life in its fullness until you overflow!" (John 10:10 TPT).

I know what some of you are thinking: *Uh...ahem...calm down, Happy Girl. Jesus was talking about an abundant life spiritually—not being all smiley and joyful!* Are you sure? If you struggle with the idea God wants you to enjoy life outside of your spiritualness (new word), let's talk about it.

God knows you are a spirit, and He wants you to enjoy abundance spiritually—but you're not a disembodied spirit. He also gave you a soul and a body through which He wants you to enjoy life and glorify Him. Wouldn't it be weird for your spirit to be happy and full of joy, and your soul and body to be grumpy, anxious, and exhausted? You would be an incongruent person.

Think about it in the natural. Would it "glorify" a parent who had a moody, unhappy, depressed kid who never laughed, smiled, or enjoyed life? Of course not. No wonder people who don't know the Lord question our Heavenly Father when they see so many of His kids being discouraged, angry, and cynical. Imagine the glory God gets when you are enjoying life—the abundant life full of joy!

Maybe you are still not convinced. You may have to renew (renovate) your mind to this truth, especially if you were raised with the idea that God is a killjoy. He's not killing joy; He's giving it!

It's a gift from God to live a full, holistic, joyful life—after all, Solomon, the wise guy from the Old Testament, told us, "People

should eat and drink and enjoy the fruits of their labor, for these are gifts from God" (Ecclesiastes 3:13 NLT).

Of course, God's not endorsing the "pleasures of sin" found in immoral, unethical, or ungodly behavior counter to His Word—He doesn't want us to be gossipy, gluttonous, covetous, materialistic, immoral drunkards who do and say hurtful things (*#obvi*). God has something better. Actual life!

What if God is okay with you smiling, laughing, dancing, ordering lobster, eating a banana split, enjoying a hike in the mountains, going on a cruise, and riding a roller coaster? He is. If you need to up your joy game, here are a few tips.

## get around joyful people

Do you hang out with happy people? Or Debbie Downer and Grumpy Greg? As the saying goes, "Show me your friends and I'll show you your future." It's true. If your cronies don't spark joy in your life, you may need some new friends. Find people who are positive. Uplifting. Fun. Find people who bring out the best in you. A good place to find people with bliss is in your local church.

I love what Brian Houston, global senior pastor of Hillsong Church, posted on Instagram (@brianchouston): "The starting point for building great relationships is making wise decisions about who we allow close to us. We need people who will build us up and take us forward, and good friends will do just that."

It's impossible to be around negative, sarcastic, critical people day after day and maintain your joy. There's no shame in saying, "Bye, bye, bye" to unhappy people in order to reinvent your friendship circle.

For many years, one of the core values at our church has been

"Life is short. Church should be fun." In other words, compared to eternity, life on earth is short—so as followers of Jesus, our lives and our church should be marked by His joy and fun.

A while ago, I posted this core value on Facebook and someone commented, "Church fun? That's not in the Bible." I found that sad. What had this person's church experience been like? Torture? Condemning? Boring? Dutiful? I understood the comment. Perhaps she thought we were being irreverent or sacrilegious.

I responded and let her know we based our belief that church should be fun on Scriptures like Psalm 16 ("In Your presence is fullness of joy; at Your right hand are pleasures forevermore") and Psalm 100 ("Make a joyful shout to the Lord, all you lands! Serve the Lord with gladness; come before His presence with singing"). I hope she took it to heart and found a church full of joy!

Joy is one of the distinguishing marks of a Christian and joy should be present in His church.

You don't have to separate your life into the sacred (where you have no fun) and the secular (where you have all the fun). No, you can live your sacred and secular life with joy—and this honors God. When you "love your life," He gets all the glory and you get the benefit!

If Jesus, the Head of the Church, was anointed with joy and if in His presence there's fullness of joy, then His church and anywhere He's present should be off the charts with joy and gladness. Basically, church should be one of the happiest and most life-giving places on earth. (Sorry, Disney!)

One of my all-time fave Scriptures is Jeremiah 15:16: "Your words were found, and I ate them, and Your word was to me the joy and rejoicing of my heart." Learning God's Word in church (and in private) should bring joy to your heart.

**start fresh. love life.**

The writer of Proverbs told us about the power of a happy heart: "A glad heart makes a happy face; a broken heart crushes the spirit" (Proverbs 15:13 NLT).

Even science is catching up to what God told us all along! In their book *How God Changes Your Brain*, Andrew Newberg, MD, and Mark Robert Waldman said:

> Smiling stimulates brain circuits that enhance social interaction, empathy, and mood. In fact, smiling has such a powerful effect on the brain that if you just see a picture of a smiling face, you will involuntarily feel happier and more secure. Conversely, frowning (or looking at frowning faces) stimulates feelings of anger, disgust, and dislike. In one controversial study, Botox injections into frown lines appeared to alleviate subjective feelings of depression.[4]

To have a cheerful, joyful heart is a choice and when we choose it, it brings healing to both our body and soul. To "choose joy" is a powerful thing! Some people may think joy, laughter, positivity, and being upbeat is naïve and lacking in depth. It's not. Joy is a strength.

I know. I've told you many of my sad and awkward stories—I know what it's like to have a "spirit of rejection" and discouragement hounding you. As a young Christian, I remember wondering if all of these verses about "joy" were for real or just the greatest-sounding theory.

I can happily report, the joy of the Lord is a real thing!

The Lord has reinvented my life in this area and by His grace, joy is my default. That doesn't mean I've had a charmed life without challenges. Like you, my husband and I have faced

many storms over the years, but we've learned that putting our trust in the Lord and leaning into His joy is the only way to survive. His perfect peace guards our hearts and minds, and that gives us the freedom to laugh and enjoy life right in the middle of big storms (like when my husband had a pulmonary embolism and the doctors asked him if he wanted to be revived or when a neighbor called to tell us our newly built house was on fire or when we were betrayed by people we trusted . . . all the normal stuff of life!).

Even when the storm winds are blowing, the joy of the Lord *is* our strength. We know and believe God loves us (remember?) and we know how the game ends—we win. This is not theory. This has been our reinvented reality for many years now. The same thing is available for you!

I love the fact that Jesus is a joyful person; turns out, He is the *most* joyful person of all! The Bible tells us because Jesus loved righteousness and despised evil, God anointed Him with the oil of joy *more* than anyone else! Here's how the Passion Translation puts it: "For this reason, God, your **God, has anointed you and poured out the oil of bliss on you** more than on any of your friends" (Hebrews 1:9 TPT).

Anointed with the oil of bliss! (I like the sound of that. Who doesn't want two pumps of anointed bliss oil in their morning coffee?) Here's the best part. The joy Jesus has, He wants to give us! Jesus said, "These things I have spoken to you, that **My joy may remain in you, and that your joy may be full**" (John 15:11).

Jesus promised joy without limits would be available after His resurrection. (This is now!)

> Until now you've not been bold enough to ask the Father for a single thing in my name, but **now you can ask, and**

> **keep on asking him**! And you can be sure that you'll receive what you ask for, **and your joy will have no limits**! (John 16:24 TPT)

Does that excite you? It should. Be bold in asking the Lord for the things you desire and allow Him to give you joy without limits. As we sometimes say (with all due respect), it's time to *get your ask in gear*—and live a joy-without-limits kind of life!

These are just a handful of Scriptures on joy. The Bible is loaded with God's desire for His children to live life—in abundance, to the full, until it overflows! Depending on what translation of the Bible you use, you'll notice words like *joyful*, *cheerful*, *bliss*, *mirth*, *merry heart*, *rejoicing*, *gladness*, *happy*, *laughter*, and other descriptions peppered throughout the Bible. All of these tell us about the relationship God wants to have with us and the life He wants us to en**joy**. (There it is again!)

Ready to enjoy life? You have God's permission:

> Teach those who are rich in this world not to be proud and not to trust in their money, which is so unreliable. **Their trust should be in God, who richly gives us all we need for our enjoyment.** Tell them to use their money to do good. They should be rich in good works and generous to those in need, always being ready to share with others. By doing this they will be storing up their treasure as a good foundation for the future so that they may experience true life. (1 Timothy 6:17–19 NLT)

See a theme? Trust in God. Be generous. Enjoy life.

Happy people have common traits. They're not always cracking jokes, although they do know how to laugh at them. They don't take themselves too seriously. They have a humble,

flexible, and easygoing nature. There is a playful spontaneity about them. They enjoy life! Does this describe your life? Would you like it to?

God wants this for you and here's where you have an advantage. The fact that *heaven wants you happy* in your reinvention journey makes answering Reinvent Question #4 easy. And here's the best part—you get to enjoy God's goodness, His blessings, and "the good life" because you *aren't* seeking those things to fulfill you—you are enjoying those things because you're already fulfilled in knowing Jesus and being focused on His cause.

When you received and welcomed Jesus as your Lord, you were set free from the shame, guilt, and condemnation of sin—and that made *e'rything* in life a whole lot sweeter! You can live your Monday–Sunday life with a joyful gusto because God loves you and Jesus took care of your core sin problem at the cross. You can praise God for your salvation and at the same time enjoy a sunset trip to the beach, a piece of apple pie, or a new bicycle from a fulfilled place of being satisfied in Jesus, not from an empty or desperate place of hoping those things would fill the void within.

Heaven wants you to love life! So go ahead, cheer up! Be glad, rejoice, laugh! Taste and see that the Lord is good. Love life with your spouse. Take your kids to the park. Get the boat. Buy the purse. Build that cabin in the woods. Enjoy a vacation with your friends. Update your kitchen. Have your cake and eat it, too! It's true—you can reinvent. You can start fresh and love your life!

> When at last your dream comes true,
> life's sweetness will satisfy your soul. (Proverbs 13:12 TPT)

Ta-da. The End. (I mean, The Beginning!) *#happydance*

## reinvention review

1. How does the idea that *heaven wants you to love life* inspire you to reinvent?
2. In what ways will you step up your joy game?
3. Knowing God wants you to cheerfully reinvent, start fresh, and love life—what top five takeaways from this book give you the most joy?

# conclusion

# reinvent: start fresh and love life!

Congratulations! You did it!

You've completed *Reinvent*.

Now it's time to start fresh and love life!

We've been on quite a journey together as we've examined the story of the Maven, taken time to uncover the 4 Reasons to Reinvent, and drilled down to answer the 4 Questions to Reinvent.

I have mixed feelings about coming to the end. You've been in my heart the entire time I've been writing, and I've thoroughly enjoyed our time together in these pages.

I pray the Lord has spoken to your heart many times and given you insights, tools, strategies, and practical how-tos that empower you. I hope you feel energized and equipped with the ingredients you need to create your own reinvention secret sauce, your customized reinvention roadmap, and your strategic reinvention game plan! Remember, no matter where you're at in life, God's specialty is reinventing the last, the least, and the lost and turning them into the first, the favored, and the found!

Now it's time to go: Reinvent. Start fresh. Love life.

I'll be here cheering you on!

But wait, there's more. One more thing.

## the most important reinvention

We've come this far together, and I wouldn't feel right if I didn't take a few moments to remind you of the most important reinvention of all—being born again and coming into a relationship with Jesus.

If you already know Jesus—great!

If not, I'd love the honor of leading you to Christ.

If you've never received Christ or confessed Jesus as the Lord of your life, now is the perfect time. You can experience an eternal reinvention right this moment by praying this prayer from your heart:

> Dear God, I realize I am a sinner in need of a Savior. I want to turn away from my own ways of living and my own efforts of self-righteousness. I humbly turn to You, Jesus. You paid a very high price by shedding Your blood on the cross to rescue me from an eternity that would be dead and apart from You. Today, I surrender my life to You. I want to be a Christian. I want to follow You. Jesus, I choose You. I believe, receive, and confess You as the Lord of my life. Thank You for forgiving me of all my sins and reinventing my life. From this moment on, I declare Jesus is the Lord of my life. I am a Christian—a Christ-follower. Help me, Lord, to start fresh and love the life You've given me. Thank You, Lord. In Jesus's name. Amen!

Finally, remember as you intentionally change, rearrange, and reinvent:

Things change,
People change,
Places change,
Friends change,
Careers change,
Economies change,
but
God never changes.

# final words

I'm so glad we've had this time together and I hope you'll stay in touch!

I'd love to hear your reinvention story. Please drop me a line and let me know how it's going as God helps you to *Reinvent: Start Fresh and Love Life!*

I can't think of a better way to say goodbye—ta-ta, ciao, and so long for now—than by praying this prayer over your life:

> I ask God to give you complete knowledge of his will and to give you spiritual wisdom and understanding. Then the way you live will always honor and please the Lord, and **your lives will produce every kind of good fruit**.
>
> All the while, you will grow as you learn to know God better and better. (Colossians 1:9–10 NLT)
>
> *In Jesus's Name. Amen!*
>
> Let's stay connected!
> **Website:** thebasicswithbeth.com
> **Facebook:** /thebasicswithbeth
> **Instagram:** /bethjones
> **Online Courses:** thebasicsuniversity.com
> *Use discount code REINVENT to get 20 percent off.*

# acknowledgments

Writing a book is like having a baby! Being pregnant with a message is one thing, but giving birth to a happy, healthy baby book is quite another!

I'm thankful that I've been blessed by hundreds of people—family, friends, teachers, mentors, authors, speakers, and pastors—whose words God used to conceive this book within me. I'm thankful for the opportunities I've had that shaped my own life and helped the contents of this book grow, develop, and come to full term.

I am most grateful for the following people who helped me deliver this book and bring it forth. No doubt, without their help, I'd still be pregnant with a half-written manuscript. Because of their help, I hope you enjoy reading this bundle of joy.

I want to give a big thanks to Ben Ferrell, my literary agent—your unflinching belief in me is the reason this book exists! You opened the door so I could work with the fabulous team at FaithWords!

Thank you, Rolf Zettersten and the amazing FaithWords/Hachette team. I enjoyed working with you all and loved your energy and "get it done" attitude.

Thank you to my editor, Virginia Bhashkar. When I sent you the first few sample chapters and held my breath to see what you'd say, your kindness and complimentary words helped me

to relax and write the rest! It was a joy to work with you. Your wisdom, insights, editing expertise, patience, and kind suggestions made this a better book!

To Luria Rittenberg, thank you for your expertise in managing the editorial process; and Carrie Andrews, thank you for your detailed work in copyediting.

Thank you, Patsy Jones, Jeana Ledbetter, Laini Brown, Rudy Kish, and Katie Norris for believing in this book and giving it life with your best ideas!

To Edward Crawford, thank you for your patience as we went back and forth on cover design ideas—I love where we landed; you nailed it!

I could not have written this book without the phenomenal people at Valley Family Church and *The Basics With Beth*—especially Amanda Harrison, Jennifer Cole, and Tara Farrell.

Amanda, thank you for answering the hundreds of midnight emails, reading the book multiple times (at 1:00 a.m., after you got your kids to bed!), and giving me your thoughtful feedback! Thank you for being a wise sounding board and making me delete things I thought were funny—but weren't. You truly helped to make this a better book. The afternoon laughs and eye rolls will never be forgotten!

Jennifer, thank you for sitting with me for several days at a time to go over each page of the manuscript and offering your fresh perspective and wise suggestions. Thank you for cheerfully volunteering to help me with the boring job of putting together the citations. You saved me days of time! (I owe you!)

Tara, besides being the best executive assistant we could ask for, your ability to know what I need and when I need it amazes me—I am especially thankful that you knew when to deliver a triple grande Americano to keep me writing. I also appreciate your help in improving the book by offering fresh input on key sections.

# ACKNOWLEDGMENTS

I would like to give my heartfelt thanks to each of these people who made this book better...

I can't put into words how thankful I am for the encouragement I received from my friends, partners, and our beloved Valley Family Church board, staff, and church family. Thank you, Wendy Treat, for your friendship. Thank you, Bruce Barton, for your on-time, God-touched words of encouragement. Thank you, Euchre Club, for cheering me on.

I feel like the luckiest (most blessed!) person in the world to have praying friends—thank you, prayer warriors: Mary Jo Fox, April Wedel, Jennifer Palen, Kathy Marble, Tonya Nielsen, Mandie Roberts, Ashley Purry, Amethyst Vineyard-Crouch, Micaela Ziegler, Jennifer Palthe, Angela Garrison, Pam Roe-Vanderberg, Barb Williams, Karen Spangler, and VFC Prayer Teams.

A special thank you to Meghan Hock and Hannah Spangler for their inspiration and the diagrams in the book.

A big huge thanks to all of you who allowed me to tell your stories in the book. You are an inspiration to others and no doubt about it, your stories made this a better book. I hope I did you good.

Thank you to my friends and ministry colleagues who were extremely gracious and wrote such nice endorsements for this book. I admire you all and truly appreciate your support, vote of confidence, and kind words.

I want to give special thanks to my mom, Carol Barker, and my dad, Jerry Shepard. Now in heaven, I'm grateful for and honor them both. And to my sisters, Rhonda Rogers, Kelly Albert, and Michelle Snow—we pretty much reinvented our childhood and a lot of our lives together. You three are the best! I'm still the big sis and I love you girls!

Thank you to our kids living all around the world—Meghan, Brodie, Annie, Zack, Luke, Kelsey, Eric, and Alexa—for your

words of encouragement, funny texts, and enthusiasm throughout the process. (Thanks, Meghan, for your helpful input on various versions of this book! Thanks, Eden and Bram, for giving Gramma a diversion and going to the petting zoo and apple orchard!) Love you all!

To Jonesie, our teacup poodle—I can't imagine writing this book without you sitting on my lap and licking my fingers at the end of a long day of typing. How did we get the best dog in the whole world?

I saved the best for last! To my husband, Jeff Jones—no one helped me with this book more than you! How can I thank you enough? Thank you for taking care of me and *everything else* for months (okay, well, actually throughout our entire marriage) so I could sit at my computer and write for days on end. Thank you for reopening Big Daddy's Bistro and making me the world's best keto-friendly breakfast every day (with extra bacon!). Thank you for doing all the laundry, all the dishes, and all the grocery shopping and never complaining when I was lost in my thoughts and writing another chapter. On top of that, thanks for reading the manuscript, in every variation, and telling me it was good—even when it was rough, confusing, and not yet organized. Thanks for always providing comic relief and declaring, NYTBS! I am the most blessed woman to have you; I love you, lovey!

Finally, my highest thanks and all the praise goes to the Lord. Thank you, Father, for the revelation of Your great love! Thank you, Jesus, for being my Lord and Savior and reinventing my life in many areas and multiple ways. Thank you, Holy Spirit, for helping me write this book to encourage others to reinvent, start fresh, and love life! I pray that eternal fruit for Your honor and glory will result in the lives of those who read these pages. Thank You, Lord!

# notes

## chapter 2: the fruit is sparse

1 Paul Roberts, "You're never too old and it's never too late," *Features Magazine* by *RI Magazine*, May 18, 2017. http://chefirvine.com/magazine/youre-never-too-old-and-its-never-too-late.

## chapter 5: you're a hero on a journey

1 "MJ on Tiger: 'Greatest comeback I've ever seen,'" ESPN, April 18, 2019. https://www.espn.com/golf/story/_/id/26553414/mj-tiger-greatest-comeback-ever-seen.
2 Dr. Lanny Johnson, "Lanny Johnson Fischbone Final," YouTube, September 1, 2017. https://www.youtube.com/watch?v=BWbRisrzrxo.
3 Dr. Lanny Johnson, "Answering the frequently asked question (FAQ) of what am I up to now," Dr. Lanny Blog. https://drlanny.com.
4 Dr. Lanny Johnson, "Life and life," Dr. Lanny Blog. https://drlanny.com.

## chapter 6: you're the best fixer-upper on the block

1 "22 ways Joanna Gaines is reinventing shiplap for 2017," *Fixer Upper,* HGTV, December 13, 2016. https://www.hgtv.ca

/shows/fixer-upper/photos/22-ways-joanna-gaines-is-reinventing-shiplap-for-2017-1053097/.

2 "G3339—metamorphoō," Blue Letter Bible. https://www.blueletterbible.org//lang/lexicon/lexicon.cfm?Strongs=G3339&t=KJV.

3 "G342—anakainōsis," Blue Letter Bible. https://www.blueletterbible.org//lang/lexicon/lexicon.cfm?Strongs=G342&t=KJV.

## chapter 8: it's better than you thought

1 Dr. Timothy Jennings, *The God-Shaped Brain* (Inter-Varsity Press, 2017), p. 27.

## chapter 9: meet the maven

1 "Maven," vocabulary.com. https://www.vocabulary.com/dictionary/maven.

## chapter 10: it's okay to want what you want

1 Dr. Caroline Leaf, "People pleasing: How it can damage your mental health and how to stop," Dr. Leaf, September 1, 2019. https://drleaf.com/blogs/news/people-pleasing-how-it-can-damage-your-mental-health-and-how-to-stop?_pos=1&_sid=b47701332&_ss=r.

2 "G2309—thelō," Blue Letter Bible. www.blueletterbible.org/lang/lexicon/lexicon.cfm?Strongs=G2309&t=KJV.

## chapter 12: go after a new bullseye

1 Dr. Maxwell Maltz, *Psycho-Cybernetics* (New York: Prentice Hall Printing, 1960).

2 Larry Alton, "Why low self-esteem may be hurting you at work,"

NBC News, November 15, 2017. https://www.nbcnews.com/better/business/why-low-self-esteem-may-be-hurting-your-career-ncna814156.
3 Dr. Maxwell Maltz, *Psycho-Cybernetics* (New York: Prentice Hall Printing, 1960), p. 16.
4 Dr. Timothy Jennings, *The God-Shaped Brain* (Inter-Varsity Press, 2017), pp. 63–65.
5 Dr. Caroline Leaf, "You are not a victim of your biology," Dr. Leaf, October 3, 2018. https://drleaf.com/blogs/news/you-are-not-a-victim-of-your-biology?_pos=1&_sid=16aa54db3&_ss=r/.

## chapter 13: go small and stay home

1 Seth Godin, *Small Is the New Big: And 183 Other Riffs, Rants and Remarkable Business Ideas.* (New York: The Penguin Group, 2006).
2 Nathan Bransford, "Amanda Hocking and the 99-cent Kindle millionaires," Nathan Bransford, March 7, 2011. https://blog.nathanbransford.com/2011/03/amanda-hocking-and-99-cent-kindle.
3 Kevin Kelly, "1,000 true fans," The Technium, March 4, 2008. https://kk.org/thetechnium/1000-true-fans/.
4 Seth Godin, "It's all horizontal (and books went first)," Seth's Blog, May 21, 2019. https://seths.blog/2019/05/its-all-horizontal-and-books-went-first/.
5 Gesine Bullock-Prado, *My Life from Scratch: A Sweet Journey of Starting Over, One Cake at a Time* (New York: Broadway Books, 2009).

## chapter 14: go big and work on your magnum opus

1 "Magnum opus," Merriam-Webster. https://www.merriam-webster.com/dictionary/magnum%20opus.
2 "Michelangelo Buonarroti quotes," Goodreads. https://www.goodreads.com/quotes/1191114-the-sculpture-is-already-complete-within-the-marble-block-before.

3 "Michelangelo," Biography. https://www.biography.com/artist/michelangelo.
4 Jessica Stewart, "12 facts you need to know about Gaudi's Sagrada Familia, Barcelona's most visited attraction," My Modern Met, May 26, 2017. https://mymodernmet.com/sagrada-familia-facts-gaudi/.
5 "Beethoven's Magnum Opus," *Serenade Magazine*, December 20, 2018. https://serenademagazine.com/series/music-education/beethovens-magnum-opus/.
6 "The Mona Lisa, Leonardo da Vinci," Futurmuseum.com. https://www.futurmuseum.com/the-mona-lisa-leonardo-da-vinci.html.
7 E. B. White, *Charlotte's Web* (New York: HarperCollins Publishers, 1952).
8 Adam Lashinsky, "Larry Page: Google should be like a family," *Fortune*, January 19, 2012. https://fortune.com/2012/01/19/larry-page-google-should-be-like-a-family/.
9 Bill and Melinda Gates, "2015 Gates Annual Letter: Our big bet for the future," Gates Notes. https://www.gatesnotes.com/2015-annual-letter? page=0&lang=en&WT.mc_id=01_21_2015_AL2015-GF_GFO_domain_Top_21.
10 Caroline Leaf, "The believer's voice of victory," May 23, 2015. https://www.youtube.com/watch?v=PAGcxLoozzw.
11 "Blaise Pascal quotes," Goodreads. https://www.goodreads.com/quotes/801132-there-is-a-god-shaped-vacuum-in-the-heart-of-each.

## chapter 15: possessions and quirks

1 Maeve McDermott, "Odd duck to diva: How Susan Boyle became an unlikely star 10 years ago," *USA Today*, April 22, 2019. https://www.usatoday.com/story/life/music/2019/04/11/susan-boyles-iconic-i-dreamed-dream-performance-turns-10/3426767002/.
2 Tyler McCarthy, "Susan Boyle explains why she was relieved to be diagnosed with Asperger's syndrome," *Fox News*, June 4, 2019. https://www.foxnews.com/entertainment/susan-boyle-aspergers-syndrome-relieved.

3 "Chariots of Fire," Quotes. https://www.quotes.net/movies/chariots_of_fire_1994.

4 Arthur Anderson, *An Actor's Odyssey: Orson Welles to Lucky the Leprechaun* (Atlanta: BearManor Media, 2010).

5 Paul Vallely, "Peter Mark Roget: A man of words," *Independent*, June 27, 2002. https://www.independent.co.uk/arts-entertainment/books/features/peter-mark-roget-a-man-of-words-181860.html.

6 Morgan Greenwald, "40 amazing things people have accomplished after 40," BestLife, July 16, 2018. https://bestlifeonline.com/accomplished-after-40/.

7 World Science Festival Staff, "10 things about Albert Einstein you didn't know," World Science Festival. https://www.worldsciencefestival.com/2015/11/10-fun-albert-einstein-facts/.

8 "Weird quirks of geniuses," Memorise. https://memorise.org/brain-articles/weird-quirk.

## chapter 16: passions and purpose

1 Dixita Limbachia, "Chick-fil-A named the #1 fast-food restaurant in America," July 6, 2018. https://www.usatoday.com/story/news/2018/07/06/chick-fil-named-number-one-fast-food-restaurant-america-texas-roadhouse-number-1-full-service/763445002/.

2 Hayley Peterson, "'Chick-fil-A is about food': How national ambitions led the chain to shed its polarizing image," Business Insider, August 6, 2017. https://www.businessinsider.com/chick-fil-a-reinvents-itself-liberal-conservative-2017-5.

3 Susan Dunne, "Ex Black Panther Jamal Joseph brings film 'Chapter & Verse' to Hartford Library," *Hartford Courant*, June 7, 2016. https://www.courant.com/ctnow/movies/hc-jamal-joseph-harford-library-20160607-story.html.

4 Mark Miller, "Artist Jamal Joseph gets prize for his own third act," Reuters, November 15, 2015. https://www.reuters.com/article/us-column-miller-purposeprize/artist-jamal-joseph-gets-prize-for-his-own-third-act-idUSKCN0T21LG20151113.

5 Jane Royer, "Beautiful people in the second half of life,"

Encore. https://encore.grfoundation.org/blog/beautiful-people-in-the-second-half-of-life.

6 Marianna Cerini, "#TBT: An exclusive interview with fashion icon Vera Wang," *That's Magazine*, October 12, 2017. https://www.thatsmags.com/shanghai/post/2236/exclusive-interview-the-yin-and-yang-of-vera-wang.

7 Bill Murphy, Jr., "14 inspiring people who found crazy success later in life," Inc. https://www.inc.com/bill-murphy-jr/14-inspiring-people-who-found-crazy-success-later-in-life.html.

8 "At 72, this ultra-marathoner continues to break records," NBC Miami, May 5, 2017. https://www.nbcmiami.com/news/local/At-72-This-Ultra-Marathoner-Continues-to-Break-Records-421512633.html.

9 Tina Daunt, "Medical marvel: At 51 woman becomes oldest graduate at USC," *Los Angeles Times*, June 1, 1992. https://www.latimes.com/archives/la-xpm-1992-06-01-me-363-story.html.

10 www.thebasicsuniversity.com

## chapter 17: friends and cronies

1 "Robin Dunbar: We can only ever have 150 friends at most...," *Guardian*, March 14, 2010. https://www.theguardian.com/technology/2010/mar/14/my-bright-idea-robin-dunbar.

2 "22 heartwarming stories of true friendship that will make you call your bestie," *Reader's Digest*, https://www.rd.com/advice/relationships/stories-of-friendship/.

## chapter 18: family and kinfolk

1 "Surrounded," Valley Worship playlist, Spotify. https://open.spotify.com/artist/2S6XE61FgatXlR4OSIEOp0?si=tqu9udlLQratf_3IGSwy1g.

## chapter 19: go, get this party started

1 Maurice Dubois, "103-year-old runner Julia 'Hurricane' Hawkins breaks new record," CBS News. https://www.cbsnews.com/news/julia-hurricane-hawkins-runner-breaks-new-record-2019-06-19/.

2 "Ben Carson quotes," Brainy Quote. https://www.brainyquote.com/quotes/ben_carson_490147.

3 Bob Goff, *Love Does: Discover a Secretly Incredible Life in an Ordinary World* (Nashville: Thomas Nelson, 2012).

4 "25 top daily YouTube vloggers," IZEA, May 16, 2018. https://izea.com/2018/05/16/daily-youtube-vloggers/.

5 James Altucher, "FAQ on how to become an idea machine," January 6, 2015. https://jamesaltucher.com/blog/faq-on-how-to-become-an-idea-machine/.

6 Marguerite Ward, "Warren Buffett's reading routine could make you smarter, science suggests," CNBC Make It, November 16, 2016. https://www.cnbc.com/2016/11/16/warren-buffetts-reading-routine-could-make-you-smarter-suggests-science.html.

7 "And the winners of the 8th Annual Eclipse Awards are . . . ," The Eclipse Award. https://www.theeclipseaward.com/.

## chapter 20: borrow, baby, borrow

1 Briana Hansen, "16 of the most inspiring rags-to-riches stories," Work + Money, March 14, 2018. https://www.workandmoney.com/s/inspiring-self-made-millionaire-d766a865d6dd45d8.

2 Gautam Naik, "A hospital races to learn lessons of Ferrari pit stop," *Wall Street Journal*, November 14, 2006. https://www.wsj.com/articles/SB116346916169622261.

3 Bogdan Popa, "Samsung wants to reinvent the past with foldable clamshell smartphone," Softpedia News, June 27, 2019. https://news.softpedia.com/news/samsung-wants-to-reinvent-the-past-with-foldable-clamshell-smartphone-526545.shtml.

4 "HRE Wheels and GE additive reinvent the 3D printed titanium wheel," 3D Printing Media Network, May 23, 2019. https://www

.3dprintingmedia.network/hre-wheels-ge-additive-3d-titanium-wheel/.

5 "History," Cirque Du Soleil. https://www.cirquedusoleil.com/about-us/history.

6 Christina Green, "11 ways Cirque Du Soleil reinvented the circus," *Event*, September 21, 2018. https://www.eventmanagerblog.com/cirque-du-soleil-reinvented-circus.

7 Catherine Clifford, "How Starbucks' Howard Schultz went from the projects to building a $3 billion fortune," CNBC Make It, June 26, 2018. https://www.cnbc.com/2018/06/04/rags-to-riches-story-of-starbucks-howard-schultz.html.

8 "History of board sports," ActionSportsVideos.com. http://www.actionsportsvideos.com/histsurf.html.

9 Megan Willett, "10 ingenious reinventions of everyday products," Business Insider, April 16, 2014. https://www.businessinsider.com/reinventions-of-everyday-products-2014-4.

## chapter 21: shut the door and pour

1 Tim Tebow, *Shaken* (New York: WaterBrook, 2016), p. 129.

## chapter 22: ring the bell and sell

1 Seth Godin, "7 ways to reinvent yourself," SUCCESS, February 1, 2017. https://www.success.com/7-ways-to-reinvent-yourself/.

2 Kathleen Elkins, "From waiting tables at Red Lobster to a $300 million fortune: The rags-to-riches story of Daymond John," Business Insider, February 25, 2016. https://www.businessinsider.com/daymond-john-rags-to-riches-story-2016-2.

3 Jane Wells, "How this entrepreneur went from a crack addict to a self-made multimillionaire," CNBC Make It, September 20, 2017. https://www.cnbc.com/2017/09/20/how-mypillow-founder-went-from-crack-addict-to-self-made-millionaire.html.

4 Alyson Shontell, "The life and awesomeness of a surfer-

turned-billionaire, GoPro founder Nick Woodman," Business Insider, June 26, 2014. https://www.businessinsider.com/the-life-and-awesomeness-of-a-gopro-founder-nick-woodman-2014-6.

5 "Our story," The Perfect Card Box, https://theperfectcardbox.com/pages/our-story.

6 "At SIR Home, we don't stop at improving your home—we're out to improve the world," SIR Home Improvements. https://www.sirhome.com/sir-home-cares/.

7 "From bottle to beautiful," Rothy's, https://rothys.com/.

## chapter 23: heaven is counting on you

1 Justin Taylor, "How much do you have to hate somebody to *not* proselytize?" The Gospel Coalition. https://www.thegospelcoalition.org/blogs/justin-taylor/how-much-do-you-have-to-hate-somebody-to-not-proselytize/.

## chapter 24: heaven is cheering you on

1 "You're not home yet," Tony Cooke Ministries. https://www.tonycooke.org/stories-and-illustrations/not_home_yet/.

## chapter 25: heaven wants you to love life

1 "Jonah and the whale," CleanJoke.com. https://www.cleanjoke.com/humor/Jonah-and-the-Whale.html.

2 "You have to spell a word to get into heaven," Reddit. https://www.reddit.com/r/Jokes/comments/5gvoqx/you_have_to_spell_a_word_to_get_into_heaven/.

3 "H2421—chayah," Blue Letter Bible. https://www.blueletterbible.org//lang/lexicon/lexicon.cfm?Strongs=H2421&t=KJV.

4 Andrew Newberg, MD, and Mark Robert Waldman, *How God Changes Your Brain* (Ballantine Books, 2009).

# about the author

**Beth Jones** is a Bible teacher, pastor, and author who has been helping people apply God's Word to reach their potential for thirty years. Her flagship book, *Getting a Grip on the Basics*, has sold more than 250,000 copies worldwide and has been translated into nineteen other languages. Her *The Basics With Beth* television program airs on several networks internationally, including Hillsong Channel and TBN Nejat in the Middle East. Beth and her husband, Jeff, founded Valley Family Church in Kalamazoo, Michigan, in 1991, and they still serve there as senior pastors. She is a podcast host and teaches thousands online through the *Basics University*. Beth and Jeff have four grown children and two grandchildren and live in Kalamazoo.